A PRACTICAL STEP-BY-STEP GUIDE

fuchsias

A PRACTICAL STEP-BY-STEP GUIDE

fuchsias

CAROL GUBLER ● NEIL SUTHERLAND
consultant: JENNY HENDY

PUBLISHED BY
SALAMANDER BOOKS LIMITED
LONDON

This edition published in 2001 by Salamander Books Limited,
8 Blenheim Court, Brewery Road,
London N7 9NY, United Kingdom

Some of the material that appears in this book was previously published in *A Creative Step-by-Step Guide to Growing Fuchsias*, also by Carol Gubler.

ISBN 1-84065-317-5

Printed and bound in Italy

CREDITS

Series consultant: Jenny Hendy
Designed and edited by: FOCUS PUBLISHING,
The Courtyard, 26 London Road, Sevenoaks, Kent TN13 1AP
Designers: Ruth Shane, David Etherington
Editors: Guy Croton, Caroline Watson
Photographer: Neil Sutherland
Editorial director: Will Steeds
Production: Phillip Chamberlain

THE AUTHOR

Carol Gubler has been involved with growing fuchsias since her early years, when she helped her father look after his increasing collection of plants in the greenhouse. She has been a member of the British Fuchsia Society Committee since 1985.

THE CONSULTANT

Jenny Hendy is a respected garden writer and author. With a lifelong passion for gardening, she has been sharing her knowledge of planting and design for the last fifteen years, through writing, lecturing and TV appearances. She now also runs a successful garden design consultancy.

THE PHOTOGRAPHER

Neil Sutherland has more than 25 years' experience in a wide range of photographic fields. His work has been published in countless books and magazines.

Half-title page, title page and contents page: All photographs by Neil Sutherland.

CONTENTS

THE BASICS

INTRODUCTION

Fuchsias are some of the world's favourite plants. With their incredible diversity and generally hardy dispositions, they can be planted in any number of different situations and environments and will flourish with relatively minimal care. They offer spectacular colour and form and will grace any garden with their distinctive flair.

Fuchsias are wonderfully adaptable plants. In the wild, they flourish in mountainous areas with a damp and humid climate. In our gardens and containers, they will thrive in a range of different conditions, as long as they receive a little shade and a touch of humidity. The simple form of the natural species has been extended by hybridization into a spectacular range of delightful cultivars. Fuchsias became extremely popular during the late 1800s, and it was then that a great deal of hybridization took place, particularly in the UK and Europe. Today, fuchsias are grown and loved throughout the world. This part of the book opens with a close look at the diversity of fuchsias available today, from the traditional hardies, with their small, delicate flowers but incredibly robust growth, to the exotic, double-flowered varieties that grace countless tubs and hanging baskets during the warm months of the year. Attention then focuses on the practical aspects of growing these glorious plants to perfection, from choosing a good plant in the first place to exhibiting prized specimens at a competitive show. Of course,

there is plenty of hard work to be done between these two points, and this section provides all the advice necessary to achieve perfect results, with full coverage on soils, planting techniques, feeding and watering, pruning, pests and diseases, winter care, propagation, pinching out, potting up and hybridizing a new variety. In fact, everything to enable even the newest beginner to grow fuchsias with confidence and success.

Right: *Fuchsia* Leverkusen *growing strongly in a container.*

Below: *The lovely double blooms of Ballet Girl.*

THE DIVERSITY OF FUCHSIAS

Fuchsia flowers are found in all sizes, from tiny blooms just 6mm (0.25in) long
to others measuring 13cm (5in) across. Flowers may be long, thin
and elegant or saucer-shaped, and vary from small and dainty singles
to large and exotic doubles with a mass of petals.

There are flowers that drip from arching branches and flowers that look you in the eye. The range of flower colours is vast and increasing, and includes white to almost black, green and almost brown. The array of shades and subtlety is breathtaking: on the one hand, pale and demure and on the other, so gaudy that the colours almost seem to clash. In an ideal situation, fuchsias can remain in flower for twelve months, although they do appreciate a short rest at some stage!

Colour is not just limited to the flowers; foliage also occurs in all imaginable shades of green. Some leaves have a matt finish, while others have a glossy sheen. Many fuchsias have variegated foliage that can include grey, cream, yellow, pink and bronze in all kinds of combinations. This variation in foliage helps to create a splash of colour long before the plants are in flower.

Sample the delights of this exotic, but easy-to-grow flower and you will never be disappointed. There is something for everyone in the extraordinary family of fuchsias, so be adventurous, and do not be constrained in ways that you might have been in the past with

other, less versatile plants. Take into account the differences in growth among fuchsias, their varying degrees of hardiness, the fact that they can be used in all sorts of containers, and you can see how flexible they are. The choice is yours: you can dabble by buying in plants every year and starting from scratch or get more involved trying some of the ideas that you will find in this book.

Above: *Single-flowered fuchsias are delightfully simple; most have four petals or, very rarely, five. The simplicity of their flowers shows their closeness to the original species.*

Far Left: Peter Bielby is a large, flamboyant, double-flowered fuchsia. Doubles have more than eight petals, often with a number of small petals, or petalloids. Some fuchsias have only five to eight.

Left: Space Shuttle is a single, but has the shape of a triphylla. It has the most unusual colour combination in its flowers, with an exceptional amount of yellow. It flowers quite easily for the whole year.

Antigone, a cultivar introduced in the 1880s.

Alison Patricia has upward-facing flowers, which is unusual among the fuchsias.

Elfriede Ott is a triphylla with typical long, thin flowers.

The deep violet flowers of Swanley Gem fade only slightly once opened.

Left: A small group of fuchsias to illustrate their diversity. They are all singles, but nevertheless they show a wide variation in shape, size and colour.

SPECIES FUCHSIAS

Modern cultivated fuchsias have opened up a whole new world, but the widespread and longstanding fascination with fuchsias was inspired by these incredible original varieties. We can learn a lot about the cultivated forms by having a look at the Species – the range that have been found is quite amazing.

Knowing something of the origin of a plant gives you many clues to growing the modern cultivars to best advantage. Fuchsia species are found in the wild in a limited number of countries, particularly in Central and South America, over a range of about 10,000 km (6,250 miles), from northern Mexico south to Argentina and Tierra del Fuego, and across the

Pacific to Tahiti and New Zealand. They occur predominantly in mountainous areas or on the edge of rainforests. Only deep into the Southern Hemisphere do they venture out onto the slopes and valleys. The first species were discovered in the 1800s and today there are over 100 known species, and more new ones are found every year. The plants come in all shapes and sizes, from large and treelike species, such as *F. arborescens* and *F. excorticata*, to those that creep, such as *F. procumbens*. The flowers occur in the size range 6mm–7.5cm (0.25–3in) and, like the cultivars, show a tremendous range of forms. Colours vary from white through orange, green and deep maroon, to the more conventional red and purple. The New Zealand species are especially fascinating, as both the flowers and foliage vary most widely from the accepted view of a fuchsia. Their growth habits include a tree form, a crawling form and a shrubby type, yet all are true fuchsias! Species are becoming increasingly popular as growers examine the sources of today's hybrids and recreate some of the early crosses that form the foundation of modern fuchsias.

Above: *This is another species fuchsia from Peru* – F. boliviana *var.* luxurians 'Alba'. *When it is in full flower, it can bear up to 40 flowers on one stem. This exceptionally strong grower can reach 1.2–1.5m (4–5ft) in one season.*

Left: *The delicately scented flowers of* F. arborescens *resemble lilac and grow in a terminal cluster.*

Right: Fuchsia fulgens rubra grandiflora *has incredible flowers up to 10cm (4in) long. It is a native of Mexico and will make a fine large plant that will thrive in a spacious container. There are a number of forms, but this is the easiest to grow.*

Above: Fuchsia denticulata, *with its beautiful, vivid flowers, was originally found in Peru and Bolivia and is easy to grow. The plant has a shrubby growth habit with blue-tinged foliage and throws up suckers around the main plant.*

Above: Fuchsia procumbens *is one of the few species found in New Zealand. It has a prostrate habit. Pink fruits follow the flowers. This fairly hardy species is a delightful subject for a rockery, as its foliage and flowers will grow freely outwards, spreading across the stones.*

THE TRIPHYLLA HYBRIDS

The triphyllas are a most distinct group of fuchsias that resulted from early crosses with *F. triphylla*, and as a group, they are vital to any fuchsia grower's collection of plants. They offer certain advantages over other groups of fuchsias and are good for creating varied displays in the garden.

The triphylla types are distinguished by a number of features: their distinctive, richly coloured foliage varies from almost a metallic bronze to a rich purple sheen and their flowers have a long thin tube and range through pink, orange and red. They are able to succeed in a much more sunny and hot environment than most other fuchsias, and this allows them to occupy a wider range of positions in the garden.

Triphylla fuchsias thrive in large pots and tubs and will flower without a break for many months, given regular feeding and watering. Triphyllas are also very easy to grow. They do best in a stress-free environment that is neither too wet nor too dry; either extreme will cause them to lose their lower leaves. During the winter, keep the temperature above 7°C (45°F). Cut them back as you would any other fuchsia and they will soon grow again. Do not treat triphyllas as hardies unless you live in a warm area.

Right: *A large container of Thalia – possibly the best known of the triphyllas. It is easy to grow and will thrive in a large container.*

Triphyllas are characterized by dark to bronze-coloured foliage and terminal flowers borne in clusters.

Above: *Traudchen Bonstedt shows clearly that the flowers are borne on the end of the branches. This relates them to the original species, F. triphylla. Even though many hybrids have been produced, they still retain the characteristics of the parent species.*

TRIPHYLLA HYBRIDS

Bornemann's Beste; Coralle; Elfriede Ott; Gartenmeister Bonstedt; Leverhulme; Mary; Schonbrunner Schuljubilaum; Thalia; Traudchen Bonstedt; Trumpeter.

Top: *Elfriede Ott is another more modern triphylla. It is unusual in having semi-double rather than single flowers – that is, five to eight petals, not four. Its lax, dangling growth makes it suitable for hanging baskets, in which it looks spectacular combined with other forms.*

Above: *Bornemann's Beste is another strong grower with terminal flowers. It will flower continuously for more than three months if you feed and water it conscientiously.*

Right: *Sophie's Surprise, the first variegated triphylla, has typical flowers but most unusual foliage. From this it is hoped to produce many more variegated triphyllas.*

Above: *Mary, one of the darkest triphyllas, has dark foliage and rich scarlet flowers. It was first introduced in Germany in 1894, one of many hybrids produced by Herr Bonstedt, who specialized in triphylla crosses.*

19

HARDY FUCHSIAS

Many fuchsias are described as hardy, which means that they survive the winter planted out in the garden in cool temperate climates and come up again the following year. The advantage of these plants – like any hardy plants – is that they generally require little care and are suited to many different environments.

Right: Beverley, a lovely vigorous grower, is another modern hardy. It is a single, with large, bell-shaped flowers. Modern hardy fuchsias are normally test-grown in a cold area to determine their hardiness.

Strong colours in hardy fuchsias flowers are ideal to brighten up a dull area of the garden.

Cultivars are only considered to be hardy when they are planted in the ground and allowed to form a natural shrubby shape; a basket or a standard will not be hardy, even though the cultivar may be considered as such.

To a great extent, your climate will dictate what is hardy. In areas that are subject to regular frosts, and where fuchsias in the garden are regularly reduced in height, you will be more limited in your choice of plants. For example, you may buy a standard fuchsia described as hardy, only to find that in cooler climates it will be knocked back and only grows as a bush the following year.

If you are uncertain as to what will be hardy in your area, make enquiries at a specialist fuchsia nursery, garden centre or local fuchsia society. And

Above: Reading Show, first introduced in the 1970s, has medium to large flowers of a good rich colour.

Right: There are many hardies with interesting foliage and Sharpitor is one of the best. It has a delightful combination of foliage and flowers. This was a chance find in the garden of a National Trust property in western England.

remember, it is always worth experimenting, as you will often be surprised by what will survive. Generally speaking, neither triphyllas nor large exotic doubles will survive if planted out in cooler climates with a number of frosts during the winter. Put these subjects in a frost-free environment for the winter to be safe.

If you are going to experiment and find out what is hardy in your garden, always make certain that you have a second plant or some cuttings that you can nurture in a frost free environment. It is always a good idea to have a second plant as your insurance policy!

Right: Mr. A. Huggett is one of the first fuchsias to flower and gives a fine display for many months. Most fuchsias have an identifiable hybridist, but this one was found by chance.

HARDY FUCHSIAS

Dwarf: Alice Hoffmann; David; Lady Thumb; Son of Thumb; Tom Thumb.
Medium: Dorothy; Garden News; Margaret Brown; Rufus; Tennessee Waltz.
Tall: Edith; Margaret; Mrs Popple; Rufus; Whiteknights Pearl.

STANDARD FUCHSIAS

Fuchsias look wonderful grown as standards; elevated on a stem you can enjoy the beauty of their flowers and their elegance so much more. It is an ideal way of looking at fuchsias with upright flowers, as the vertical form of the standard mirrors the orientation of the blooms and enhances the overall effect.

The basic requirements for growing a standard are a good, straight stem, a well-formed head and a good covering of flowers. Use a trailing cultivar and you will have a lovely weeping standard. You can grow any variety of fuchsia as a standard, although some plants will require much more effort than others.

Never grow a standard that will be taller than you can easily manage to keep through the winter. Be wary of proportion; a large flower on a short standard will look odd, as will a very small head on a very long stem. Small flowers on small standards look much better. Always bring standard fuchsias into a frost-free environment for the winter months in cool temperate climates, otherwise you could end up with a bush rather than a standard. The stem can easily be caught by a cold spell, as there is no protection for it. All it needs to survive the winter is a warmer environment.

Check in the spring that the standard has survived by gently scratching the stem. If the layer under the bark is green then it has, and if the conditions are right the fuchsia could survive for many years to come.

Above: *Royal Velvet, a fine old cultivar. The weight of the large double flowers gives it an almost weeping shape. This type of growth may need extra support, such as tying the branches to a central cane.*

Left: *A young, first-year standard of Reg Gubler, a fuchsia named after the author's late father. Being a first-season plant, the head is still small. Next year it will be larger and bushier.*

Right: Shelford has been one of the most popular cultivars during the last few years. It flowers continuously for many months and is easy to shape. The shadier the planting position, the whiter the flowers will be. In a sunny spot, the flowers are almost pink.

Below: Silver Dollar is a lovely white cultivar. Including plants at the base of a standard can considerably improve its appearance. The plants also help to keep the fuchsia cool by shading its roots.

The kink in the stem is unfortunate, but not so serious that it will cause a weakness in the plant's support.

FUCHSIAS FOR HANGING BASKETS

A hanging basket of fuchsias creates a wonderfully elegant garden feature. When the basket is in full flower, it should be an absolute cascade of blooms. Whether the fuchsias you choose for your hanging basket are single-flowered, double-flowered or grown for their foliage, they will all produce equally phenomenal results.

To achieve the ideal effect, which is for the growth to obscure the basket and have flowers cascading all over it, always use the same cultivar in one basket. If you use different fuchsias within the same basket, it will look messy and unbalanced.

There are many basket cultivars available, all of which should have a lax style of growth. It is an ideal way to show off the very large doubles; the weight of their exotic blooms makes them ideal candidates for a basket hanging at a level where they can be seen. Single-flowered fuchsias, with their multitude of flowers, will also show themselves well in a basket. With these, you are more likely to achieve the ideal basket, with blooms right from the top to the bottom as a glorious waterfall of colour.

Remember that fuchsias look equally good in half baskets, whether they hang on the house or against a garden wall or fence. However, beware of placing any basket of fuchsias in a very sunny spot, as the warmth from a building can literally cook them. Place them on the shadier side and you will achieve far better results.

Above: *Waveney Gem is one of the most adaptable fuchsias. Not only does it grow into a superb basket, it can just as easily be grown into a standard, a large pot plant, a fan or a pillar. Its brilliant pink and white flowers are instantly recognizable wherever it is grown.*

Careful attention throughout the summer will keep a basket like this in continuous flower for many months.

Above: *Red Spider makes a good basket, festooned with flowers for many months. Do not be deterred by the fuchsia's name, which may remind you of red spider mite; it produces an enchanting basket with ease.*

Above: *An ideal basket cultivar is one that drips with flowers from top to bottom and where the depth of foliage is such that you cannot see the basket at all. Wilson's Pearls is an excellent example, with lovely, rich, semi-double blooms.*

Right: *Abigail is a beautiful Dutch cultivar, with exceptionally shaped flowers that open out into a saucer shape. To see it at its best, view it from below rather than from above.*

25

TOP TIPS FOR HANGING BASKETS

It is difficult to go wrong with fuchsias in hanging baskets. Unlike many other plants suitable for this growing medium, they are unfussy and relatively easy to look after. However, there are a few golden rules you should follow for consistently successful hanging baskets featuring fuchsias, as follows.

- Plant all the same cultivar in a basket for the best effect – a mixture will generally produce an unbalanced and untidy-looking container, as fuchsias all grow differently.
- Ensure that the hanging basket gets regular watering during the summer months, as a basket that it is full of growth and possibly full of roots can dry out very quickly indeed. If this is the case, you could try adding water-retaining granules to the compost in the hanging basket, but this is really only advisable in hot sunny spots.
- Feed your hanging basket regularly. This will promote good growth and continual flowering during the summer. Use either a feed that you can water in or the slow-release fertilisers that you add to the compost when you first make up the basket.
- Remove all seed pods and dead flowers at least once a week to maintain lots of flowers in the basket.

Wilma Verslot is a vigorous fuchsia with a trailing habit which is ideal for dramatic hanging baskets like the one shown here.

- If the spot turns out to be too hot, find a shadier area to prevent the fuchsia basket from suffering too much and wilting in the heat.
- Wilting can mean either 'I need a water' or 'I am suffering in the heat'. Check by feeling the compost. If it is dry, it needs a water. If it is wet, find a cooler spot for the plants to recover in!
- Check that the basket has good drainage. A moss-lined wire mesh basket may need a small plastic base to help retain the water – with a few small holes to give it some drainage. The man-made basket liners now available are sometimes better than moss.
- If the basket is swinging in a windy spot, watch out for plant damage: fuchsias can be fragile!
- If you have not got room for a proper basket, try hanging pots. These can look just as good and will probably need only one fuchsia in them.
- To get a good structure and lots of flowers stop the plants every three pairs of leaves for the best results.

Below: *Tom West is an outstanding fuchsia with shiny foliage and a habit which lends itself perfectly to hanging baskets.*

BEST CULTIVARS

Singles: Abigail; Aunty Jinks; Daisy Bell; Hermiena; Jack Shahan; Marinka; President Margaret Slater; Red Spider; Waveney Gem.

Doubles: Applause; Blush O' Dawn; Dancing Flame; Devonshire Dumpling; Frau Hilde Rademacher; Malibu Mist; Pink Galore.

Above: *La Campanella will make a fantastic hanging basket, providing many months of flowers. The tube and sepals are white with a slight hint of pink, the petals are dark purple. The flowers are semi-double, medium sized and produced in profusion. La Campanella will grow and flower well in both a sunny and shady spot in the garden.*

BUSH FUCHSIAS

The most common and the easiest way of growing fuchsias is as a bush, as this is most like the form in which they would naturally grow. Fuchsia bushes are always striking, with strong form and invariably dramatic flowers. There are many different reliable cultivars available.

Plant a fuchsia in the garden and nature will produce a neat, bushy plant, which will fend for itself and not require regular attention. However, a plant in a pot does need some control and this is done by regular stopping – that is pinching out the growing tips to shape the plant.

Ideally, a bush should be reasonably symmetrical and have an even development of growth and flowers. Pinching out gives the plant a good structure that will form the basis of its subsequent development. A good shape and structure will result in a plant that is full of flower and pleasing to the eye.

If you feed and water the plant regularly it will give you many months of flowering pleasure. Fuchsias repay good care, although they don't need much. Once you have mastered the technique of shaping a bush fuchsia, you can try other forms. Basket and standard fuchsias, windowboxes, tubs and bedding are all shaped in the same way. Once again, variety and being adventurous are the keys to success!

Left: *Tom Thumb is best known as a dwarf hardy, but is bush-shaped. If a bush is defined as a plant with many branches but no trailing growth, then Tom Thumb is a fine specimen.*

Right: *Jenny Sorenson is a delightful single-flowered fuchsia with delicate banding around the edges of the petals. It branches out well, making for good coverage, and has a stiff growth habit.*

Right: Voodoo is a double with large flowers borne on strong stems. Unlike many doubles that need to grow in a position where they can trail, Voodoo will develop into a fine bush, producing a good number of splendid flowers.

Right: Annabel has almost white, large, showy flowers, but they are not too heavy to weigh down the stems of this sturdy bush. Pinch out regularly.

TOP TIPS FOR BUSH FUCHSIAS

Fuchsias will grow vigorously in pots and tubs in the garden,
but there are always things you can do to help them fulfil their best potential.
Here is a collection of hints and tips designed to ensure that you get
the best from all your bush plants.

- A bush fuchsia grown in a pot needs regular stopping to get all round growth and lots of flowers. Stop after every two pairs of leaves for a compact shape; however, if you prefer a looser style of growth then stop after three pairs of leaves.
- Remember: it takes approximately 60 days from final stop to full flowering for a single fuchsia, 70 days for a semi-double, 80 days for a double and 100 days for a Triphylla!

Above: *Gartenmeister Bonstedt is a wonderful triphylla that will give many months of flowering during the summer. Remember that Triphyllas are happy in a more sunny spot than most other fuchsias. Fuchsias in pots must be given protection against the cold during the winter; if not, the roots can be frosted and this will kill the plant.*

Left: *Herald growing with viola. This is a favourite fuchsia that will grow into an enormous plant when planted in a large container! Use low growing plants such as viola to add to the charm of a tub.*

CULTIVARS OF BUSH FUCHSIAS

Singles: Bill Gilbert; Border Queen; Carla Johnson; Jenny Sorenson; Love's Reward; Mission Bells; Nellie Nuttall; Pink Fantasia; Shelford; Taddle.

Doubles: Annabel; Brookwood Bell; Eusabia; Heidi Ann; Marcus Graham; Paula Jane; Ridestar; Spion Kop; Topper; Voodoo.

- Feed and water to maintain a healthy plant.
- Fuchsias in small pots in the sun can often suffer from scorching of the roots. Either move them to a shadier spot or place them in a larger pot for a 'double glazed' effect – with the roots in the shade.
- Remember to turn the pots at least twice a week so that the growth is much the same on all sides.
- Bush fuchsias can be kept and grown for many years. Cut them back in the autumn to maintain a good shape.
- Regular removal of dead flowers, seed pods and yellow leaves will not only make your plant look better, but also will ensure that it flowers for longer.
- With so many fuchsias to choose from, try a few different ones every year; look out for those that do well in your area.

Above: Galadriel is a small flowered single. In full flower it will be a mass of bright flowers that sparkle. It is a short jointed plant and will make a wonderful small bush ideal for the front of containers or a bed.

Right: Waveney Sunrise has the bonus of not only its delightful two-tone pink flowers but gorgeous yellow green foliage as well. Use plants like this to lift the colour in a dull area. The colour of the foliage will be dictated by the amount of shade the plant is grown in – more light, more colour!

FUCHSIAS FOR FOLIAGE

When considering which fuchsias to plant, it is tempting to choose varieties purely for their flowers, but why not consider the beauty of their foliage? There are many cultivars of fuchsias with ornamental and variegated foliage just waiting to be discovered.

Foliage fuchsias will add colour to your garden long before they are in flower. They are all mutations, or sports, from a cultivar with ordinary green foliage. This means that any flowers they produce will tend to be smaller than the parent cultivar, as they are in reality a weakened form of the original. Even so, the flowers and foliage together will really enhance the plant. The old foliage fuchsias tend to have red-purple flowers, whereas the more modern ones can bear any type of flowers, from small singles to large, exotic doubles. When they flower, the effect can be stunning. Some of the earliest variegated fuchsias originated in the 1800s and are still very popular. Today, with the great influx of new cultivars in the last 20 years or so, the number of ornamental-leaved fuchsias has increased dramatically. As well as the variegated-leaved fuchsias, why not add even more to your colour

Right: Tricolor, a strong-growing garden hardy with three distinct tones to its leaves, will brighten any flowerbed. This old cultivar is a variegated form of F. magellanica.

Above: F. magellanica aurea *is a golden form of the strong-growing hardy. It is just as tough and will give its best golden colour when planted in a shady spot.*

Above: Golden Marinka, a variegated form of the lovely old basket cultivar, has deep red single flowers. It will also make a graceful basket plant.

Right: Autumnale, or Burning Bush, has glowing gold and red leaves and grows strongly. It will fill a hanging basket or flourish in a pot.

Right: The variety Tom West was first discovered in 1853. This absolutely delightful fuchsia, with its shiny foliage, is ideal in hanging baskets and troughs.

range with the triphyllas and their dark velvety leaves? Or try *F. magellanica aurea*, with its lovely golden foliage that will make a bright splash of colour. The depth of the foliage colour will be enhanced by growing the plants in the shade and, as usual, by good and regular feeding. The variety Tom West will become much pinker in the shade, while Genii is much more yellow. Foliage fuchsias are ideal for growing in any sort of container, as they will add colour and variety to your planting schemes all year round.

Popsie Girl is a variegated form of Orange Drops, with a matt finish to its foliage. The flowers are bright orange. Examine your plants closely for any change in the foliage; Popsie Girl was found in this way.

FUCHSIAS FOR FOLIAGE

Every collection of fuchsias should include some with attractive foliage. Good choices include the following varieties:
Cloth of Gold;
F. magellanica aurea;
Genii; Golden Marinka;
Ornamental Pearl;
Pop Whitlock;
Sharpitor; Sunray;
Tom West; Tricolor;
Tropic Sunset.

33

CHOOSING A GOOD PLANT

If you are just beginning to investigate the world of fuchsias, you will want to find the best places to start or increase your collection. There are a number of options, but a specialist nursery has to be the best. Try Yellow Pages or look at the listings pages of gardening magazines for those local to you.

Garden centre staff will be able to advise you about choosing the most appropriate varieties and how to grow them. Garden centres can also be good sources of plants, but the range of varieties may be limited. Finally, it is always worth investigating local plant sales, where gems are often to be found, even if they are not correctly named. There are various points to look for before you actually buy a plant. Firstly, examine it closely to make sure it is healthy. If the plant dies within a few days of purchase, then the chances are that it was not healthy at the nursery. It is very much a case of buyer beware; look under the leaves and at the stem for any possible damage or pests. For example, if the base of the stem is a shiny brown, it could be that the plant has had problems with botrytis at some stage, and the stem will always have a weakness, so look for another plant.

Above right: *Look underneath leaves as well as on top for signs of pests or disease. Plants with yellow leaves may be potbound or underfed.*

Left: *This specimen of F. arborescens has healthy foliage, has been well-shaped and promises more attractive blooms in the future.*

GOOD PLANTS

TAKING A CHANCE

The only time you might wish to consider buying a plant that looks in dubious condition is if it is a variety that you are desperate to acquire. In that case, take a cutting for insurance as soon as can. If the original plant has a poor shape, cut it hard back. The new growth should be healthy and you can improve its shape by regular stopping. If you suspect that the plant is incorrectly named, wait until it is in flower before seeking expert advice.

Above: *This fine bushy fuchsia will make a good plant. It has been regularly fed, turned and pinched out.*

Left: *A fine bushy, healthy plant immediately catches the eye. A nursery selling plants as good as these is well worth a visit.*

BAD PLANTS

There are signs of rust on the leaves of this plant. This problem spreads quickly and could affect your other plants.

This plant has been stopped once and is becoming straggly. It may have had too little light and has also become potbound.

This plant has been pinched out too far up the stem and is a poor shape. It would be hard to do much constructive with such a plant.

A thoroughly neglected plant without even a hint of shape. It might be worth taking cuttings from it.

A generally neglected plant with signs of rust. A hard pinch back will improve the shape and a fungicide will prevent the return of rust.

This larger plant has been stopped once and then allowed to grow on. The branch on the left has lost leaves, perhaps due to damping off earlier on.

CHOOSING THE RIGHT SOIL

There are many planting mixtures available; some are peat-based, others contain loam, coco fibre or even bark. Fuchsias are very amenable and will grow in any medium, as long as it is free-draining and contains nothing harmful which could destroy the plants' equilibrium.

Look in your garden centre or nursery at the many products available. A premixed product from one of these outlets is an excellent choice, as it contains everything your plant could need, including feed. Check that stocks are fresh; old mixtures tend to smell damp, musty and stale.

Making up your own potting mixture is probably the best option; not only will it always be fresh, but you will know exactly what it contains. The main ingredient of a planting mixture should be a growing medium, such as peat, to retain moisture and nutrients and allow for drainage. You will also

Below: Traditionally, fuchsias were grown in a loam-based medium. This is a much heavier product than the others and ideal for plants in an exposed situation and buffeted by winds.

In many areas, peat-based mixes are still easy to obtain and are an excellent basis for a planting mixture. They are soft and extremely fibrous and they retain water and nutrients well. Fuchsias thrive in this medium.

Mixtures that contain no peat are increasingly popular. This one is made up of bark and other woody material. Some contain coco fibre, cocoa shells and even paper waste.

Terracotta pots are slightly porous and ideal for all fuchsias – particularly the triphyllas that prefer drier conditions.

Fuchsias do well in plastic pots, but shade the roots. If necessary, put the pot inside a larger one; the air trapped between the two pots keeps the roots cool.

WATER RETAINING GEL

1 Add the granules to water and leave them until they expand into a glutinous mass.

Above: *When grown in a suitable rooting medium, a plant will soon develop a collection of small, fibrous roots and a central tap root. Healthy roots are white with very tiny hairlike protrusions that increase their surface area and their ability to take up food and water.*

need a product to open up the growing medium and increase drainage; this could be some kind of grit, coarse sand or perlite.

Finally, you should add a slow-release fertilizer, which is available as a prepackaged product and contains an excellent balance of ingredients, including trace elements, to promote healthy growing plants. It may be sold as a general fertilizer that you add to the potting mix; if in doubt, ask for advice, as there are many products to choose from. Keep the potting mixture dry to prolong its useful life.

2 Add the required amount of gel to the soil. Too much gel could cause waterlogging.

Add one 15cm (6in) potful of grit to every bucket of peat and other fibrous planting mixtures. It improves drainage and adds weight.

Perlite is a very good alternative to grit for improving drainage in peat-based mixtures. Being light, it is ideal for hanging baskets.

Vermiculite is able to retain water, as well as open out the texture of a planting mixture to improve drainage. Add it on its own or together with perlite or grit.

Slow-release fertilizers added to the basic mixture are an excellent way of ensuring that your plants receive vital nutrients. Use a liquid feed as well.

3 Mix the gel in thoroughly, carefully following the manufacturer's instructions.

37

PLANTING HARDY FUCHSIAS

Fuchsias are ideal for borders in the garden and, once established, will delight you for many years. When you have chosen the planting area, add some humus and some slow-release fertilizer to the soil to encourage the plants to grow well in their first season.

Before planting out hardy fuchsias, make sure you know how tall they are likely to grow, and base your planting plan around those heights. Nurseries and garden centres will be happy to advise you if you are in doubt.

Planting is a simple operation, but be sure to follow it up correctly. Water your plants regularly during the first season to help them establish a good root run, which is vital for their survival. After the first year, watering will depend on your local climate. Never water a plant when it is in full sun, as water splashed onto the leaves could cause them to scorch and burn. One way to reduce the need for watering is to apply a mulch, such as chipped bark, around the plants and this also helps to keep down weeds. An occasional feed during the first season helps to build up a plant so that it can survive its first winter.

Before the onset of the colder weather, give your hardy fuchsias a little extra protection, either by earthing them up or by placing straw or some other suitable insulating medium around the plant. This will keep them warm, which is particularly important during their first winter in cool temperate climates.

Below: *Position your plants carefully to allow them plenty of room to grow. Plant the shorter ones at the front and the taller varieties at the back. There are fuchsias to suit every aspect.*

White Pixie, a red-and-white single.

Brutus, an old single cultivar.

Nicola Jane has large double flowers.

Pink Goon, a lovely double. (The same variety is planted at bottom right.)

Son of Thumb, a shorter grower.

F. magellanica aurea

Alice Hoffmann has rose-and-white semi-double flowers.

1 *Remove the fuchsia from its pot. Put some peat in the base of the planting hole. Plant the fuchsia 2.5cm (1in) deeper than it was in the pot.*

2 *Support the fuchsia gently while you fill in the hole with the excavated soil. Take care not to damage the rootball. Water the fuchsia before planting it out.*

3 *Press the soil down gently with your hands. Make the area around the actual plant slightly higher, as this will help the plant survive the winter.*

4 *Water the plant without getting moisture on the leaves. Keep the newly planted fuchsias well watered during their first year, while they establish a good root run.*

5 *Add a little mulch around the plant. This retains the moisture in the soil and reduce the chances of any weeds growing around the plant and competing for nutrients.*

FEEDING AND WATERING

Maintaining a regular feeding programme during the year will make all the difference to general growth and flowering. As discussed earlier on, fuchsias are relatively hardy and forgiving plants, but they will always benefit from attentive care, repaying your efforts with healthier looks and a more robust habit.

Well-fed, healthy foliage has a good, strong colour.

Put the feeding pellet in the pot near the rootball. A large container, such as a hanging basket, may need two or three pellets.

***Left:** Slow-release pellets have become very popular. Feed is released from the tiny capsules over a period of months. This is ideal for hanging baskets and tubs that are not always easy to feed.*

The feeding routine can be quite simple: every 10–15 days in spring, use a high-nitrogen feed with a proportion of 25:15:15 (nitrogen: phosphate: potash) to encourage healthy growth. Never apply a stronger mix than is recommended by the manufacturer; too much high-nitrogen feed can result in soft, lush growth.

Change the feed in late spring to encourage the plant to begin producing flowers. Aim for a balanced feed with a proportion of 20:20:20 and stay with this until the end of the flowering season. Again, never overdo the quantity of feed in any one week. If you prefer, feed the plants with the fertilizer diluted to quarter strength four times a week or twice a week at half strength, for example. Simply choose a plan that suits you best.

If flowering is a little slow, it can be worth using a feed, such as a tomato fertilizer, that has a higher potash content, that is 15:15:30. However, good daylight and regular, balanced feeding should be sufficient to produce a plant that is full of flower. Water fuchsias individually, as some will require vast quantities and others seem to need very little.

Above: *Keep powdered feeds in a closed container, as they take up moisture from the air. Keep the feeding programme simple – your plants will be the better for it.*

Above: *Liquid feeds are very popular. Follow the instructions on the bottle and do not be tempted to feed more than a full dose. It is much better to feed plants at half strength twice a week than to overdo it.*

Above: *Yellowing leaves are often linked to a lack of feed. Give plants a general balanced feed with a variety of trace elements.*

Above: *A lack of water results in soft, limp leaves and wilted growing tips. Water the plant gently and empty the saucer after 30 minutes, rather than leaving the plant standing in water.*

WATERING FUCHSIAS

Overwatering causes as many problems as underwatering. A very wet fuchsia will look as limp as a dry one – only the wetness of the soil will give you a clue. If you think a plant is too wet, place it in a cool, shady spot. If the soil is saturated, take the plant out of its pot and place it on dry paper towel to draw water out of the soil and prevent the plant from drowning.

Left: *Gentle spraying helps to create a humid atmosphere and certain feeds are also applied to plants in this way. Look for foliar feeds; with this method the plants take up the nutrients through their leaves.*

41

STARTING UP IN SPRING

The first signs of growth on a plant bring reassurance that all is well. With a little encouragement of feed and light, then the tiny bits of new growth will soon develop into small shoots that can be pinched out after two pairs of leaves and a new bush structure can be started.

If potting down to a smaller pot is not feasible, use the same size pot as before.

Potting at this stage allows you to do further potting later in the year into larger pots.

Spring growth should appear from the base of the plant to the tips of the wood. If not, prune any dead wood.

As soon as the air and soil temperatures begin to rise, your plants will be stimulated into the early signs of growth. If they have been kept in a dark environment, then any young growth will be white and straggly and will fall off soon after it has been brought out into the light. However, this will soon be replaced with healthy green shoots. Light and warmth are vital during this period of the year, and a good mixture of the two will encourage the plant to grow. Once new growth has been established, the time has come to have a close look at the plant. Firstly, has there been any dieback on the old wood? If so, lightly prune the plant again, but be sure to keep an idea of the ultimate shape of the plant firmly in mind. Spring is an excellent time to give fuchsias some fresh potting mixture to stimulate them into even more growth. If you can get the plant into a slightly smaller pot you will have an opportunity to pot it back up into a larger container later in the season. It is equally important that you begin to feed your plants at this stage; a high-nitrogen feed is the most suitable.

1 *Fuchsias kept at above 5°C (40°F) continue growing slowly through the winter. As the days lengthen, growth speeds up. Pot them into some fresh soil to give them a boost.*

2 *Even in spring this plant has plenty of healthy roots. If there are few roots, check for vine weevil larvae. Old brown roots mean the plant needs fresh potting mixture.*

3 *Remove both old roots and potting mixture with your hands. Do not worry if you damage the roots; they will soon grow back and be even stronger than they were before.*

4 *In order to fit the plant back into the same size pot or a slightly smaller one, you must be ruthless – but still leave a good mass of roots.*

5 *Place a little fresh potting mixture in the bottom of the pot. Position the plant in the pot and gently add fresh soil down the sides of the rootball. Do not press down the potting mixture.*

6 *If the potting mixture sinks down too far, add some more to the top at a later stage. Water the plant and keep it in a stress-free environment for several days.*

This variety is Auntie Jinks. It has been successfully potted down into a smaller container.

SLOW GROWERS

If a fuchsia is not growing, gently scrape off a little bark with your fingernail. If it is green underneath, the plant is alive. If it is brown, scrape another area of bark below, as the plant may have died back a little. If it is alive, it will need some extra nurturing to stimulate it into life.

Above: *Spray the wood with tepid water daily to soften the bark and stimulate the plant into growth.*

Left: *If a small standard does not grow from the top, trim off the top and grow it as a tall bush.*

Below: *If a standard is slow to grow, lay it down to make it easier for the sap to get to the top.*

TAKING A CUTTING

The best time to take fuchsia cuttings is when the growth is soft and green.
Avoid taking cuttings during the summer months, when it tends to be
harder and woody. Furthermore, once a plant is determined
to flower, it is less likely to root.

Having prepared the ideal environment for your cuttings to root and grow (see pages 46–47), the next crucial step is to choose the right plant material. If you start with a poor cutting, it is much harder to grow it into a good plant. Consequently, choose young and tender growth, as old, woody material will always take much longer to root. Remember that the growth hormones that control the plant's ability to root and grow are found in the very tip of the stem, so long cuttings will take more time to root. A good cutting should look healthy and have two leaves of the same size around the stem. The equal size of the leaves is important in order to produce a fine, balanced plant. Some plants occasionally produce stems with three leaves rather than two, and these make excellent cuttings and a far superior plant. Finally, have everything prepared before you start to take cuttings, as a delay between cutting and placing the pieces in the rooting medium of your choice can be fatal to the delicate young plants.

Right: A plant that is just starting to flower is not an ideal candidate for cutting material. The hormones in the growing tip will be directed towards flowering, rather than towards rooting.

Left: These stems are becoming woody. Cuttings taken from such a plant will take a long time to root.

This soft, healthy growth should root successfully and provide you with a supply of fine new plants.

Below: This plant is covered with young growing tips, which make excellent cuttings. In taking cuttings, you are performing two tasks at once: increasing your stocks and improving the shape of the plant by stopping it.

Always select cuttings from a good-quality, healthy plant.

1 *The ideal fuchsia cutting has a growing tip, one half-opened pair of leaves, one fully opened pair and about 1.25cm (0.5in) of clear stem.*

Cut just above a leaf joint. This will minimize the area of damage and effectively stop the plant.

2 *Use a clean sharp knife to cut the stem. Make a straight cut that does not unduly damage the stem. A cutting with a damaged stem is more likely to damp-off than root.*

3 *Hold the cutting by the leaf, rather than by the stem. Touching the stem can damage the fragile tissues of the young plant and cause problems with rooting later on.*

THE KEY TO TAKING SUCCESSFUL CUTTINGS

Always cut the stem cleanly, using a sharp knife or similar tool. A blunt cut will damage the tender tissues. Never allow a cutting to dry out, as this will greatly reduce the chances of successful rooting. If necessary, place fresh cuttings in a small container of water. If you wish, you could add an extremely dilute solution of fungicide to the water to improve the plants' chances of survival. Use only the best plant material for cuttings. Remember, the better the cutting, the better the final plant.

The growing tip need not be present for the cutting to root. This internodal cutting will root and bush out without needing a first stop.

If cutting material is in very short supply, slice the cutting down the centre. Use a sharp knife to minimize the damage; both parts should root well.

Ideally, avoid an uneven cutting, as the developing plant will also be uneven.

A three-leafed cutting makes an ideal plant, with three side shoots, rather than two.

Small cuttings root faster, as the growth hormone at the growing tip has less far to travel.

RAISING THE CUTTINGS

Fuchsias can be rooted in almost any medium, as long as it contains nothing harmful which could upset their equilibrium, but you must help them along by providing an atmosphere that will encourage rooting and growth. There are a variety of ways in which this can be done.

Propagators are available in many shapes and forms, from simple, homemade types to expensive, finely tuned commercial models. Whatever type you decide to use, they must provide three definite conditions: a humid atmosphere, the correct temperature, and an even level of light. These three factors are vital in most stages of a plant's growth, and a propagator should provide the right balance. Humidity is the most important: too dry an atmosphere will put the cutting under too much stress and it will not root; too wet, and the cuttings could damp-off, so you must aim for the right balance. Next in importance is the temperature. The majority of failures are probably caused by too much warmth; the optimum temperature is about 15°C (60°F). Finally light: the cuttings should root in an environment that is in light but not in direct sunlight; too bright, and the young cuttings will be under too much stress and fail. Once you have found the ideal growing environment for your cuttings, you should achieve success every time.

Above: You can monitor the progress of the cuttings through the clear plastic lid. The vents in the lid allow you to increase ventilation as required.

Left: A seed tray filled with small pots or trays allows you to keep a variety of cuttings in one container. Be sure to label each batch clearly.

HOMEMADE PROPAGATORS

Homemade propagators can be made from a range of household objects. They must provide a humid microclimate for the young cuttings to root and grow. Each one performs like a miniature greenhouse that you can control. Never let cuttings dry out – keep them cool and shady. Once they have rooted, open the container for a few hours each day so that they can become acclimatized to conditions in the outside world.

A glass jar will take a tray with 8–10 cuttings. Its clear sides and screw top make it an ideal propagator, but keep it out of direct sun.

A plastic bag holds a 13cm (5in) pot. Place the cuttings in wetted potting mixture and mist them well. Place a cane in the pot and secure the bag to it.

An old coffee jar over the potting mix will also create a greenhouse-type of environment for the cuttings. Be careful not to damage the delicate cuttings as you cover them with the jar.

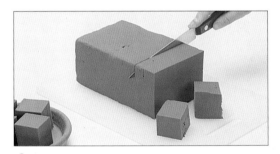

1 *Cut a block of flower foam into 1in(2.5cm) square blocks. This rooting medium retains water and creates a humid atmosphere.*

Flower foam is an ideal rooting medium containing nothing harmful.

2 *Wet the blocks of flower foam thoroughly, not only watering them from above, but also letting them soak up water from the saucer. Keep them wet at all times.*

3 *Use a fine stick or the end of a knife to make a small, shallow hole in the foam blocks to hold each cutting in position. Hold the cutting by the leaves, taking care not to damage the tender stem.*

4 *Carefully insert the cuttings into the small holes. Do not force them in, as this could damage the stem, which is where the new roots will develop over the next 10-14 days. Use the cuttings as soon as possible after you take them.*

5 *Cuttings rooted in this way can be placed directly into a suitable potting mix.*

The leaves should just clear the foam block.

47

POTTING ON AND PINCHING OUT

Pinching out or stopping is crucial to the growing plant as it gives us a chance to control the way a plant grows. The technique allows the ability to shape a plant and control the time that it flowers – but more of that later!

Left: When the cutting has grown to 2.5–5cm (1–2in), its roots should be well developed and it is ready to pot on. Remove the cutting from the propagator, holding it carefully so that you do not damage the tender young stem. Gently insert the cutting into the potting mixture.

When the young cuttings have rooted, the leaf tips become a much brighter shade of green and, without actually growing, the whole plant seems to elongate. However, this would be far too soon to move the cutting to its first pot; the average interval between taking the cutting and potting it on is one month. Weather, light and the time of year can all have an effect: it will be shorter in the spring when the sap is rising, but longer in the fall. Typically, a young plant should be about 5cm (2in) long before you pot it up. It should also have at least two fully grown pairs of leaves, plus the growing tip, and the roots should be well formed. The best time to carry out the

Always plant into a small pot, as the shock of a move into too large a pot can slow down the plant's growth until it becomes established.

This is a young plant before its first stop. At this stage, it has only one stem.

After one stop, the plant has produced a number of side shoots. They have developed from above the leaves on the main stem.

Each time you remove the growing tip on a stem, at least two branches will grow, and frequently more.

first pinch out, or stop, is much the same as for the first pot. Do not leave it until the plant is too tall, unless you are thinking of growing it as a standard or another shape. Stopping performs two vital functions: firstly, it encourages the plant to become bushy and thus controls the shape. Secondly, at later stages of the plant's development, stopping gives you some control over the flowering time, so it is well worth mastering the technique early on.

Each time you remove a growing tip on a fuchsia at least two new branches will be produced from lower down the stem. A simple mathematical progression means that within a few stops you can have a wonderfully bushy plant covered with lots of branches and masses of flowers.

HOW TO PRODUCE A BUSHY PLANT

One stem stopped once will produce at least two stems, stopped again, at least four, stopped a third time, at least eight. In a cutting with three leaves at a node, the progression speeds up. A bushy plant is easy to achieve by pinching out after every two pairs of leaves.

The young plant is ready for its first pinch out when it has grown at least three pairs of leaves. Use fine scissors or tweezers to remove the smallest portion of growing tip. This allows side shoots to grow, forming the beginnings of a bushy plant.

GETTING YOUR PLANTS INTO SHAPE

Stopping, shaping and turning are all aspects of growing fuchsias that tend to be overlooked in the desire to see them flower, but it is worth spending time on these tasks as the result will be manageable and pleasing plants.

The importance of stopping a plant is explained on page 48–49. The number of pairs of leaves between stops is a matter of personal preference – a rampant grower will need stopping after every pair of leaves, while a slower, short-jointed variety would benefit from a looser style, so stopping after every two or three pairs of leaves would be better. The decision you make will control the final shape and style of the plant. The more you stop a plant, the bushier it becomes. It also lets you control the shape of the plant, which is essential if you are growing a standard or want to control a plant with wayward growth. Turning is critical to create a fuchsia with all-round growth and flowers. Ideally, the more you turn the plants, the rounder their shape will become. Aim to turn a plant 90° every three days, or more frequently if you have the time. Turning reduces the chance of a lop-sided, flat or triangular plant – a fuchsia that is not turned will soon grow towards the light. Turning your plants regularly helps you to get to know them as individuals, so that you notice when they need a little extra attention, perhaps a little more water.

Left: *At least twice a week, turn fuchsias 90° to ensure that they develop a well-balanced shape. The more you turn them, the more symmetrical their shape will be.*

Below: *This plant has not been well-stopped and shaped during its early stages. It is leaning over and lacks the ideal bushy shape.*

Below: *This plant has been stopped on a regular basis and is compact and bushy and also shows a nice symmetrical outline.*

This specimen of Ridestar has not been turned equally and has become triangular rather than round in shape.

This example of Waveney Gem has been turned equally and regularly and has a much more symmetrical growth pattern.

Waveney Gem is beginning to show some large buds, five to six weeks after the final stop. Within two or three weeks, given good light, feeding and watering, it will be in full flower.

THE RIGHT TIMING

To get your fuchsias in full flower when you wish, you need to calculate the interval between the final stop and when they are to flower. Singles need between eight and ten weeks, doubles between ten and twelve weeks. These are only guidelines, as the weather, light, temperature and feeding may all influence the timing. Each cultivar will vary slightly, but these guidelines will apply to most of them. If in doubt, always reckon on the longer time; it is far easier to remove flowers than to try and force a plant into flower.

Above: *Waveney Gem in full flower. It will continue to bloom for many months. This lovely single-flowered fuchsia was photographed nine weeks after the final stop.*

Above: *Ridestar in full flower. It is a most delightful double with large blooms. Unlike many fuchsias with this colouring, Ridestar flowers fade very little once they have opened.*

As a double, Ridestar is lagging a little behind; it will take somewhat longer to flower, as the blooms are that much larger. Most doubles take between ten and twelve weeks to give their best show.

51

POTTING UP YOUR FUCHSIAS

Like most plants, fuchsias benefit greatly from being repotted. It is an opportunity to refresh the plant and provide it with a new growing medium. The plant will soon be encouraged to put on an extra spurt of growth and will generally look and feel healthier. It also gives you the chance to change the size or style of a pot.

The 'pot-in-pot' method shown here is an ideal way of transferring a plant from one size pot to the next with the minimum of disturbance to the rootball, thus ensuring that any effect on growth is minimal. It also reduces any damage to the top growth, as you do not have to press the potting mixture down in the pot.

There will be times when a move to a larger container is called for, such as when transferring a plant to a tub. In this case, it is probably easier to revert to the more normal type of potting technique.

As usual, take care not to press down too hard on the potting mixture. Moving standards from pot to pot is another occasion to use the traditional method. The amount of potting mixture that you put at the bottom of the pot will determine the height that your plant goes into the new pot. This can be an ideal opportunity to lower a plant that is showing bare stems and is in danger of not being properly nourished. You can put fresh soil on top of the existing rootball; this topdressing can be beneficial to the plant and encourages new growth.

1 *Keep the difference in pot sizes to a minimum. If a plant is potted on into a pot that is too large, it will start producing roots to fill the new space before producing top growth.*

2 *Put a little potting mix in the base of the larger pot and place the smaller pot on top. Trickle soil gently between the two pots. Gently push the smaller pot outwards to bind the soil.*

3 *Slowly lift the small pot out of the larger one. The soil should have formed a mould around the edges. If there is a gap or if it collapses, it is easy enough to start again.*

Wait until the rootball is well established and the plant is under minimal stress before potting on. For example, never pot on when a plant is over dry.

5 A plant that was ready for potting on always looks at home in the larger pot. Potting up by this method ensures that the plant continues growing with the minimum delay.

Always use clean pots. If necessary, wash them thoroughly before use. Failure to clean the pot can lead to the spread of soil-borne pests and diseases.

After potting, water the plant gently and keep it in a cool, shady position while it recovers from the upheaval. If the level of the soil sinks, add a little more.

4 Carefully lower the plant into the mould that you have made – a steady hand is useful! Once it is fully down, add a little fresh potting mix to the surface of the rootball. This will encourage the plant into even more new growth.

POTTING YOUR PLANTS SUCCESSFULLY

Do not pot up a plant until the roots are well established in the existing potting mixture. Never pot up a plant in full flower, as the shock could cause the plant to lose both flowers and buds. Never pot up a plant that is under stress, for example in full sun, too wet or too dry. Pot up and then place the plant in a cool, shady spot to recover. Never push the soil hard down into the pot. Modern, fibrous potting mixtures will find their own level. If they sink, just add more potting mixture to the surface of the pot. If the potting mixture is damp rather than wet it will fall into the gaps more easily. Varying the amount of mixture in the bottom of the pot enables you to lower or raise the plant in its new container. Dropping the plant in the pot allows you to hide any bare lower stems. To achieve the effect of an extra large plant, try potting three similarly sized plants into one large pot. This is an ideal way of filling large tubs and containers.

COLOUR GUIDE (1)

The next few pages are designed to give you ideas of how best to treat the various colour ranges
in fuchsia plants and how to combine different colours and plants most effectively.
Firstly, how to handle the beautiful orange fuchsias and
make the most successful planting combinations.

Colour in the garden is becoming more and more popular. You may be someone who likes to plant in a very random way, without thinking too much about colour schemes: this will work wonderfully well with fuchsias, as however hard you may try the colours found in nature never clash – they might take your breath away, but they will always co-ordinate!

On the other hand, there are many gardeners who think carefully about colour before they plant anything so that they can see how colours will combine together and therefore get a particular effect to work. If you are looking at colours in your garden, fuchsias offer such a wide variety of possibilities with a fantastic range of shades available – in fact, all the colours of the rainbow, as well as from white through to virtually black. There must be a fuchsia colour to suit every person and every place.

Hot, hot, hot! Hot colours in the garden are really popular these days and the orange fuchsias are as hot as they can get! Lighten up a dark spot or perhaps plant an area to make other red- and orange-flowered plants even brighter!

Some of the best orange fuchsias are Triphyllas, either bush or basket fuchsias, and in all cases the vivid colours will brighten up the area you are planting. Use them as a contrast with dark leafed foliage plants and they will lift the colour. In a garden where you are creating a tropical look with lots of hot colours, they will shine as brightly as any other plant. The Triphyllas all tend to have a dark-bronze purple shading to the foliage, which means that they can look spectacular before they are in flower, particularly if they are planted amongst silver leafed plants.

All the orange fuchsias that I have suggested are fairly heat tolerant – particularly the Triphyllas, which will take a fair amount of sun!

Sometimes a lighter combination of colours is needed in the garden or for your pots and containers, and then I would suggest the white and orange bicolours as these will really sparkle in a dull or shady spot. These are the sort of fuchsias that will really make an impact wherever they are placed. Try: Baskets: Sylvia Barker; Chandlerii; Frosted Flame; Bush: Celia Smedley; Lye's Unique; Antigone; Wassernymph; Amy Lye.

Above: *Adinda has probably some of the smallest flowers of a Triphylla, pale salmon orange and borne in terminal clusters.*

COLOUR GUIDE

TOP ORANGES

Really Bright Triphyllas:
Thalia;
Timothy Titus;
Insulinde.
Bush: Orange Flare;
Orange Drops;
Paulus;
Paul Berry;
WALZ Mandolin;
Laura;
Chang.
Baskets: WALZ Harp;
Dancing Flame;
Coachman.

SUBTLE ORANGES

Triphyllas: Coralle;
Billy Green;
Adinda.
Bush: Aurora;
Superba;
Joan Cooper.
Baskets: Peachy;
Marcus Graham.

ORANGE FLARE

Orange Flare has large single flowers in vivid orange with strong, upright growth. The dramatic flowers will light up any spot in your garden. Try planting it with pastel colours to heighten the effect.

ORANGE KING

Double flowers in shades of orange make this an excellent plant for a hanging basket. The flowers change colour dramatically as the bloom matures from orange through to smokey pink.

THALIA

This is probably the most popular of the Triphyllas. It has brilliant flowers and dark foliage and loves sunny spots.

55

COLOUR GUIDE (2)

Think of fuchsias, and you probably think pink – or maybe red or purple.
This is certainly the most popular of the colour ranges that fuchsias come in,
but there are so many variations on the theme that a stunning set of
combinations can be achieved with a myriad of different varieties.

Of all the colour ranges, this is the one that everyone traditionally thinks of when it comes to fuchsias. This is because these are the original, natural colours of these plants – the colours of those that grow semi-wild in so many different parts of the world.

The pink/red/purple colour group is one that covers everything from the subtle pale pinks and lilac fuchsias – such as Maria Landy and Holly's Beauty – through to the richness of the reds and purples of Royal Velvet and Grus aus den Bodenthal.

Plant the pastel pink and purple plants with other pastel colours for a cool effect. Use subtle shades for your patio or summer bedding – particularly if you are looking for that cottage garden look – or try a single shade effect using just one or two species of the same colours.

Richer colours will give your garden that touch of the exotic that every garden needs! The dramatic dark reds and purples of many fuchsias can look absolutely fantastic when planted with white or pale pink flowers. Be adventurous and go for bold combinations: nature will ensure that the colours never clash.

PINKS

Bush: Whiteknights Pearl; Leonora; Carla Johnston; Alan Titchmarsh; Doris Joan; Hobson's Choice; Pink Fantasia.
Baskets: Pink Marshmallow; Pink Galore; Mary Ellen Guffy.

PINKS AND PURPLES

Bush: Pink Fantasia; Princess Pamela; Heidi Ann; Chillerton Beauty.
Baskets: Ernie Bromley; Star Eyes; Lena.

REDS AND PURPLES

Bush: Reg Gubler; Royal Velvet; Voodoo; Grus Aus den Bodenthal; Dark Eyes; Bland's New Striped; Avalanche; Dollar Princess.
Baskets: Frau Hilde Rademacher; Janice Ann; Autumnale; Tom West – both the latter have gorgeous foliage as well!

COLOUR GUIDE

PINK GALORE

Pink Galore is an excellent basket fuchsia with large rich pink flowers and dark glossy green foliage. It will cascade with flowers all summer long. Don't forget to remove the seed pods on a regular basis.

DISPLAY

Display has been around since the late 1800s and is a wonderfully reliable fuchsia with its brilliant pink flowers and compact growth. The flowers will flare out to delightful saucer shapes.

MISSION BELLS

This fuchsia has everything: rich flowers in dark shades of red and purple velvet; petals that flare out to a saucer shape; and it is easy to grow! Mission Bells looks good in a large pot on a patio.

PINK RAIN

Pink Rain has hundreds of small flowers when it is in full flower, living up to its name! The combination of pastel shades of pink and its ease of growth makes it a great fuchsia to grow. Pink Rain is ideal for fuchsia bonsai.

LADY BOOTHBY

Lady Boothby has incredibly dark flowers. It has very strong growth – it is probably the fastest growing fuchsia that I know – and is often called the climbing fuchsia as it will grow so quickly!

COLOUR GUIDE (3)

Whites, lilacs and soft purples are the sophisticated shades of the fuchsia
world, offering scope for subtle colour combinations and softer,
more gentle highlights. There are a surprising number of different varieties
to experiment with in this colour group.

These are the coolest fuchsia colours of all. Sometimes a garden or patio can look just too vivid and bright, and fuchsias in cooler shades are the ideal plants to bring about the subtlety that a garden sometimes needs. There are no pure white fuchsias – even the whitest tend to have just a hint of pink or cream about them – but this adds to their charm and lightness. You might like to try whites on their own, or perhaps white with lilac, which brings you into a whole new world of colour combinations. Finally in this group there are the lush whites and purples – vivid, eye-catching and exuberant. Many of these blue-coloured fuchsias show quite a range in colours as the flowers mature – so the young flowers can be a vivid dark blue purple, later becoming a deep lilac. The colour range can be so wide that it almost looks as if you have more than one cultivar planted!

WHITES

Bush: Annabel;
Evensong;
Ting-a-ling;
Wigan Peer;
Hawkshead.
Baskets: La Bergere;
White King.

WHITES AND LILACS

Bush: Lillian Annetts;
Quasar;
Joel;
Impulse.
Baskets: Blue Veil;
Sailor;
Holly's Beauty.

WHITES AND PURPLES

Bush: Preston Guild;
Deep Purple;
Rose of Castile;
Estelle Marie.
Baskets: Pinto de Blue;
Dodo.

COLOUR GUIDE

ROY WALKER

Roy Walker has medium sized white double flowers with, as usual, just a faint hint of colour. Grow it in a shady spot and you will find that the flowers become almost pure white. It is great for putting into tubs and pots.

COUNTESS OF ABERDEEN

(Below:) Countess of Aberdeen has been around for over 100 years and is still one of the best white fuchsias currently grown.

DELTA'S BRIDE

Delta's Bride has petals that will go virtually back to flat saucer, so it will always create a stir. Grow this fantastic fuchsia in the shade and it would be a perfect gift for any bride!

FEY

Fey is an enchanting double fuchsia with lax growth that will make it ideal for baskets. The lilac of the petals makes it a great foil for a wide range of other summer plants. It has a creamy white tube and sepals.

THE PROJECTS

INTRODUCTION

Fuchsias in full bloom put on a superb display. It is not surprising, therefore, that these graceful flowers are extremely popular around the world for the colour and elegance they bring to containers and garden borders alike.

Fuchsias have so much to offer. There are pastel shades that blend harmoniously or vivid oranges and reds that will brighten the darkest corner. There are single-flowered plants that are almost constantly in bloom and exotic cultivars laden with fewer but larger double flowers in truly wonderful colour combinations. And, of course, many fuchsias have bright or variegated foliage to take the eye. Whichever way you look at it, as a group of plants fuchsias offer more than just about any other.

This section of the book presents a wealth of display ideas and projects to create, with fuchsias that highlight the beauty and versatility of these magnificent plants. There are pages on how to make the most of fuchsias in summer bedding schemes, containers and mixed hanging baskets. Growing fuchsias into fans, pillars, hoops, spirals and other shapes has been popular since Victorian times and the necessary growing and shaping techniques are fully covered here. This is followed by a fascinating look at growing fuchsias in unusual containers, how to raise them as bonsai specimens and simple ways to maintain them successfully indoors. We also show how to create a stylish fuchsia flower tower and how to mix fuchsias effectively in baskets, either in single fuchsia themes or with a range of other plants.

Right: *Fuchsias grace a mixed flower display.*

Below: *The exquisitely tinted blooms of Vanessa Jackson.*

SUMMER BEDDING

Fuchsias have to be at their best when they are planted out in the garden. They are much easier to maintain in this situation, needing only regular watering and feeding to give you many months of flowers and in many cases delightful foliage. Don't forget that these fuchsias will have to be brought in somewhere frost free for the winter.

Below: Although it is a double, Paula Jane has a rigid growth habit and holds its vivid ruby-coloured flowers aloft. It will brighten up the garden, particularly when it is grown alongside impatiens and lobelia.

Using fuchsias as a form of summer bedding, rather than as permanent planting, can add a whole new dimension to your garden and gives you more scope to experiment. Use standards as part of your planting scheme to increase the range of possible heights. Add further contrasts by using the larger doubles and triphyllas, but bear in mind that neither of these should be left outside for the winter months, although they will do very well during the summer. Look for good colour schemes to go with your other bedding plants, either to blend in with colours you already use or to add a contrast. For example, fuchsias can add a great deal to an orange or white area or to a pale pink one. When planting areas of summer bedding, why not try groups of three or five plants of a cultivar in one area – odd numbers always look best. Group plantings will maximize any effect that you are trying to achieve. Be even braver and try planting a whole bed with just one cultivar. There is nothing more eye-catching than fuchsia flowers en masse.

Fuchsias planted out for the summer will still need a shady spot and regular watering,

Left: Fuchsia paniculata *is a tender species and an unusual, but effective, choice for summer bedding. The large grapelike fruits that appear after flowering are very popular with birds.*

Right: *For a really eye-catching splash of colour, combine bright fuchsias with a selection of summer bedding. Here pelargoniums, ageratums and begonias are set off by the silver foliage of* Cineraria maritima. *Standards add height and depth to the display.*

Left: *Here, a traditional red-and-purple fuchsia is teamed with a dark heliotrope to provide a reasonably restrained colour scheme. Use colours to either brighten or calm an area of the garden.*

as their roots will not have had time to establish a good root run. Do not be tempted to leave them in the garden in their pots. If it is very hot, the roots will burn and their ability to take up any available water will be limited by the drainage holes in the pot.

Regular feeding is vital to maintain continual flowering. Once a week, apply a balanced feed with a ratio of 20:20:20. This will increase the fuchsias' natural desire to flower even more. Be adventurous and beautify your garden with fuchsias.

TROUGHS AND WINDOWBOXES

Fuchsias work well in most containers because they combine striking form with dramatic colours – the two main constituents of an effective container display. Many fuchsias have a spreading or trailing habit, so they lend themselves particularly well to the long, low shapes of troughs and windowboxes.

Make certain that the container provides ample drainage for the plants.

Fuchsias are ideal plants for any kind of container, be it a tub, a trough or a windowbox. Whether you plant them on their own or with other plants, such as ivy-leaved pelargoniums and brachycome, they will flower continuously for many months. To keep them looking their best, carry out regular general summer maintenance, which means removing dead flowers, seedpods, etc. Use their delightful range of flower colours to their best advantage. Try foliage fuchsias to increase your range of

Left: For something really exotic with a tropical look, try planting up a large container with a good-sized specimen of Thalia, plus Cordyline and some pelargoniums for added colour.

Right: Any kind of container can look good in the garden, as long as it has ample drainage holes. Here, a fuchsia is clearly thriving in a classic chimney pot with an open base.

Below: A nicely balanced windowbox, featuring a strong-growing, upright double fuchsia with a selection of trailing plants – Brachycome and Nepeta – to provide a contrast of shapes and textures.

Left: The plant and container should be in proportion to one another. This specimen of Thalia suits the fairly tall half-barrel and does not mind a warm, sunny spot.

Below: This delightful feature at the corner of a wall makes a focal point for the garden. To succeed, the colour of the fuchsia must complement that of the other plants and the container.

possibilities even further, as they will provide a splash of colour long before they are in flower. When planting up the container, check the drainage, as a waterlogged fuchsia will soon suffer and possibly die. If drainage is poor, improve it by adding grit, pieces of broken flowerpot or small pebbles to the bottom of the container. As with baskets, add a slow-release fertilizer at planting time. This can save you having to remember to feed your fuchsias regularly, unless you feel that the plants need a boost. Choose plants and colours that will suit you, mixing uprights and trailing varieties, if the situation will allow. If not, keep to one type only. The colours of plants never seem to clash, so let your imagination run riot!

PLANTING A BASKET OF FUCHSIAS

Most people would agree that the ideal way to view fuchsia flowers is when they are growing in a hanging basket. You can really see them in all their glory from below or, best of all, at eye level. However, a basket is not the natural environment of a fuchsia, so in this situation the plants need greater care than usual.

For the best effect, restrict each basket to only one variety of fuchsia; if you mix them, they begin to look messy, as different varieties will grow at different rates and flower at different times. Eventually, the whole effect can become untidy. The number of plants that you put in a basket depends very much on the size of the basket.

Always plant one in the middle, otherwise you can end up with a hole as the plants begin to grow downwards. The plants still need regular stopping after every two or three pairs of leaves to achieve a longer, but not straggly, look. Choose your varieties with care and you cannot fail to be delighted with the effect that your basket will give, whether it drips with enormous double flowers, or cascades from top to bottom with smaller single flowers. To ensure that the basket flowers continuously for many months, remove dead flowerheads and seedpods and feed it regularly. A slow-release fertilizer is useful if the basket is difficult to reach for liquid feeding. Remember to turn the basket regularly to make sure that it retains a balanced shape as it grows.

1 *Choose a peat-based potting medium as this will make the basket less heavy. Select a suitable cultivar for your basket and always use an odd number of plants for best effect.*

2 *Place a little potting mixture in the base of the basket and then position all the plants except one around the edge of the container in a pleasing and symmetrical pattern.*

3 *Finally add the central plant. This one will prevent a hole appearing at the top of the basket once the plants have started to grow.*

4 *Fill in the gaps between the plants with soil, but do not push it down – let it find its own level. Add a slow-release fertilizer to make feeding easier.*

Left: The basket of Ballet Girl is coming into flower 10–12 weeks after the final stop. The blooms are hanging over the sides of the basket and will soon cascade in all directions.

5 Fix the chains onto the basket, so that the plants can grow around them without being damaged. Tie the chains securely to a cane to keep them well above the growing plants.

6 After six weeks the plants have filled the basket and are beginning to trail over the sides. This basket had its final stop three weeks before it reached this stage.

FUCHSIAS IN MIXED HANGING BASKETS

When you look up at fuchsia flowers, you are seeing them as they should be viewed, so when they are planted in hanging baskets you can really appreciate the blooms. Sometimes fuchsias look at their very best when they are imaginatively combined with other plants, and baskets enable this better than any other medium.

The large doubles do superbly well in baskets, as the weight of their flowers pulls the stems downwards. Mixed baskets open up a range of possibilities, because incorporating other plants ensures a longer flowering period than a basket of fuchsias alone can offer. The mixture of plants can be very individual, allowing you to choose between, say, bright colours or a more subtle colour scheme. However, it is important to achieve the right balance of plants. For example, do not combine sun- and shade-loving plants, as one group is bound to suffer. In a mixed basket containing a number of fuchsias, select plants that enjoy a degree of shade. Modern baskets often have holes in the sides for extra plants, but do not be tempted to pack the basket too tightly, as all the plants will need space to grow. Remember that a mixed basket needs plenty of regular feeding, as the plants will all be competing for nutrients.

Below: *Generally speaking, it is a good idea to plant just one cultivar in each basket. However, a mixture of fuchsias, combined with other plants, works successfully in this display.*

Left: *The depth of colour and the size of its flowers make Swingtime, in the foreground, one of the most popular basket cultivars. Single cultivar baskets hanging together can make a striking display.*

Right: *Try contrasting as well as harmonizing colour schemes. Choose a scheme that suits you and the planting situation.*

Right: *Mixed baskets provide a wide variety of colours and textures. This one contains eight different types of plants, which means that some of them will always be in flower.*

Below: *This basket catches the glow of the sandstone wall. It contains a variety of foliage plants and Marinka, a rich red basket cultivar that flowers continuously for many months.*

Use foliage plants to enhance the effect of a mixed basket. They will give colour to the display before the basket is in flower.

CREATING A FAN OF FUCHSIAS

The Victorians were perhaps the finest exponents of this form of growing fuchsias. The oldest fuchsia books feature photographs of incredibly tall plants and show how they were carried around on carts from place to place.

Although the Victorians created fuchsia fans on a grand scale, do not let this deter you, as you need not! Fans and pillars do not have to be tall in order to be effective; smaller ones are much more manageable and highly acceptable. Coincidentally, many of the older fuchsia varieties, particularly those considered as hardies, are some of the best for growing as pillars or fans. Once the structure is established, it can be maintained for many years. In fact, the plants really mature and are often much better in their second or third season. When growing a fan, it is very much a case of looking for the right cutting, namely one that has a definite spread to it and looks as if it can be trained to the appropriate style. Stopping is again particularly important to determine the plant's shape. Pinch out the side shoots to add depth and solidity to the framework of branches. Always aim for a symmetrical, well-balanced shape. Espaliers are a similar form of growth, with one central stem and the laterals trained horizontally. You can have fun experimenting with different shapes if you find the right cutting to start with.

With its striking flowers and strong growth, Banstead Bell is an ideal cultivar for a fan.

Right: *A small fan during its first season of growth. In the course of the following season the growth will come from the old wood and the plant will be much larger than before.*

The foliage on a fan should fall right down to the pot, so that the branches are well hidden.

1 *Choose a plant of a cultivar that you know to be a strong grower. Ideally, it will have had one pinch out and have produced at least three strong-growing branches.*

2 *Insert small canes carefully into the rootball. Do not replace them until a later stage when the fan is considerably larger. Space the canes symmetrically within the pot.*

3 *Fasten another cane across the top to stabilize. If necessary, add a second cane lower down, particularly as the structure gets larger.*

4 *Gently direct the growth towards the cane, without damaging the stem. Carry out all positioning before the growth becomes hard and woody.*

5 *Use a plant tie or a soft piece of string to secure the plant to the cane. Do not tie it too tightly. Keep the growth as straight as possible.*

6 *You can produce fans in all kinds of shapes and sizes. An odd number of branches will give a more pleasing shape once they have been trained.*

7 *To create a good structure, begin stopping as the plant reaches the top of the first set of canes.*

8 *Stopping the top growing tips will cause the plant to bush out. Doing the same on the developing side shoots will result in a plant with a more solid structure.*

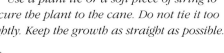

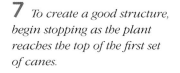

CREATING A PILLAR OF FUCHSIAS

When you have grown fuchsias for a while it is great to have a go at something that is a challenge, and trying your hand at a pillar or a pyramid will give you a chance to tackle something that was first achieved by the Victorian growers. They used to grow them up to 2.4m (8ft) tall: start smaller, and then who knows!

Try to keep the growth as straight as possible.

Pillars are perhaps easier to grow than fans, as they are very much like a standard with side shoots left on all the way down the stem. The stopping programme is once again important, as is the use of canes – both will help to produce a sound structure.

When it is finished, a pillar should be symmetrical in shape and the same width across the top as it is at the base. Another

Do not pot up the fuchsia until the roots are starting to fill the container.

1 *To start training a pillar, choose a plant that has one strong leader, preferably with a number of side shoots. Insert a cane through the centre, being careful not to damage the main stem. You can always use a larger cane later on if this one seems too small or insubstantial.*

2 *Tie the main stem of the plant gently to the central cane. It is important not to damage the tender young growth of the fuchsia at this early stage of the process, so do not pull the string too tightly against the stem and handle it gently.*

3 *Start to improve the shape by pulling the side stems into the centre. Use a soft tie to fasten them in. Do this while the stems are young and still malleable.*

shape you might like to try is a pyramid, that is, a plant that is broader across the base and coming to a point at the top. This is just as effective a shape for training fuchsias.

Once again, the basis is much as a standard and careful, regular stopping will produce a lovely and unusual triangular plant. This is not quite as easy to achieve as some methods and needs some practice, so try growing pillars and fans first and then attempt some of the

other shapes later on. It is a challenge to tackle these old ways of growing fuchsias, but it pays dividends!

Always remember that these structures will have to be kept frost free during the winter, and like standards the main stem will need protecting. In the autumn give the now woody side shoots a prune so that the shape can be maintained whilst making it more manageable to bring in to a protected area.

Below: *A large pillar of* F. magellanica aurea *just coming into flower. Try putting more than one plant in a pot like this one to achieve a large pillar more quickly.*

Pinch out the side shoots, but do not remove too much growth. The aim of the exercise is to improve the shape of the plant.

4 *Once you are happy with the form of the plant, pinch out the side shoots to make the shape more bushy. Leave the main central stem unstopped, so that it continues to grow taller to produce the pillar.*

5 *Keep on tying in side shoots until you are happy with the height and shape of the plant. Then discontinue stopping and allow the plant to flower.*

FRAMES AND HOOPS

Fuchsia growing should be fun and it is not always important that the plants are grown in conventional shapes. There are times when it is worthwhile experimenting. Many cultivars have a very supple growth that you can bring under control with a little training.

The advantage of growing fuchsias around wire or plastic shapes is that you do not have to worry about stopping times – as the plant grows, it flowers!

There are several points to bear in mind when training a fuchsia around a frame or hoop. Firstly, if you are using wire, try to use a plastic-coated kind, otherwise the heat from the wire can burn the plants during the summer months. Secondly, think about the cultivar that you are choosing. If you want a small shape, use a small-flowered type, as a large flower would look totally out of proportion. It is not always necessary to use the most floriferous cultivars, as continually tying or bending in the young growth will enhance any floral display simply because the flowers are so much closer together.

This applies particularly to the encliandras; with their extremely small flowers they can look sparse in other circumstances. Using more than one plant in the pot can make growing a three-dimensional structure much easier. Finally, do not be discouraged if you do not achieve the expected result first time; a little perseverance will certainly pay off!

Use a plastic frame or plastic-covered wire to avoid the risk of scorching growth in hot weather.

1 *Fuchsias can easily be trained into a shape while they are young and supple, so start at this stage. Add the wire before the plant has grown too large, moulding it to the required size and shape.*

2 *Use soft ties that will not damage the tender young growth. Add more ties every few days to ensure that the fuchsia is closely moulded to the wire shape while the growth is still supple. Fuchsias can grow quickly!*

MAKING SHAPES

Making shapes is as simple as bending the wire. As long as the angles are not too extreme, fuchsias will accommodate a wide range of forms. Why not try your house number or your initials? All it needs are nimble fingers and a degree of patience. Be imaginative and adventurous!

CULTIVARS FOR SHAPES

F. hidalgensis; *F. hemsleyana*; La Campanella; Lottie Hobbie; Mrs Lovell Swisher; Mrs Popple; Neapolitan; Northway; Pink Rain; String of Pearls; Topper; Whiteknights Pearl.

4 *Below: Eventually the circle is complete and Whiteknights Pearl is beginning to come into flower. Choose a cultivar with flowers in proportion to the size of the hoop. A strong grower is also useful.*

3 *The plants need no stopping, because they flower as they grow. It is important to maintain a regular feeding programme to ensure fine healthy growth at all times.*

Above: *F. hidalgensis, with its attractive, small white flowers, has been used to form this globe.*

Above: *A spiral is easy to make using the same species, one of the most supple for this purpose.*

LARGE FUCHSIAS

Take care when potting on fuchsias that have been grown in elaborate shapes. You may need a helper to balance and support the frame. Large hoops are a little flimsy until they have become established, so do not leave them in a windy position. Be sure to give these pots a full half turn to ensure that they grow evenly; a quarter turn is not enough. For the best results, tie in the growth every two or three days. This ensures that the shape remains neat.

GROWING STANDARD FUCHSIAS

People often view the prospect of growing a standard with great trepidation, whereas it is no harder or easier than any other form of growth. Virtually any variety of fuchsia can be grown as a standard: trailing varieties make a wonderful weeping head, while bush varieties result in a more traditional, but equally delightful, type of standard.

A standard is really a well-stopped plant on top of a stem that is as straight as possible. Any flaw or blemish in the stem can reduce its strength, which can cause problems if the plant is in an exposed position. It is harder to produce a very straight stem on a trailing fuchsia, as the growth is naturally more supple, but regularly tying the stem to a cane can help. When selecting a cutting to grow as a standard, try to choose one with three leaves at each node, as this will produce a superior standard to a cutting with just two leaves. Tie it onto a cane as soon as possible, so that the plant gets off to a good start. Pot the whip, as it is now called, into a larger pot as often as necessary; a potbound plant will start to flower and not grow, thus defeating the object of the exercise. The final height of a standard is up to you; generally speaking, the taller ones have more problems and can look out of proportion until they are several years old and have achieved a good size head. Bear in mind that tall standards can be difficult to store during the winter. All standards must be kept frost-free, otherwise the stem can die and you will be left with a bush the following year.

1 *Choose a cutting with a straight stem and, if possible, three leaves at each node. Carefully insert a stick into the potting mixture and prepare to tie the cutting to it.*

2 *Gently bring the cutting in close to the stick. Use a soft tie to avoid damaging the tender growth. Keep the stem as straight as possible; it is particularly supple at this stage.*

3 *Carefully break off any side shoots that appear in the axil of the leaves by gently bending them to one side. Retain the top five sets of leaves, as they will form the head.*

4 *When the young standard has reached the required height, remove the growing tip with a pair of sharp scissors. Do not remove the large leaves on the main stem yet.*

A STANDARD EMERGES

As standards develop, they need attention every few days. A plant can produce a remarkable amount of new growth in a short time. A regular care program produces better plants.

5 *Now the remaining five side shoots will start to grow. Leave them to produce two or three pairs of leaves. Pinch out the growing tips, using either a fine, sharp pair of scissors, as illustrated, or your fingertips. It is important to be as gentle as possible.*

6 *As the bushy head starts to form, remove the large leaves on the main stem, which has become quite woody at this stage. Small side shoots often appear on the main stem away from the head. Gently break them off, taking great care.*

A good, straight stem will make for a stronger standard.

7 *Now that it has a well-formed head, the young standard is ready to flower. Do not allow it to flower until it has reached this stage, as the weight of the flowers, particularly large doubles, can break the stem.*

A young standard, ready for its first stop on the side shoots.

FUCHSIAS AS BONSAI

Growing fuchsias as bonsai subjects is as much of a challenge as creating large structures.
However, fuchsias are more than happy to be root-pruned and this makes them ideal
candidates for bonsai. Why not try this unusual application for fuchsias,
once you have exhausted some of their more conventional uses?

The most important thing is to choose the right varieties of fuchsia to grow as bonsai, as the proportion of the plant to the container and the fuchsia's general growth pattern are clearly vital considerations. Large flowers on a small plant in a small pot would look quite wrong. You will have to rethink some basic gardening principles, too. For example, a plant with a balanced shape is no longer the aim. Have a look at any less than perfect plants and you may well find a potential bonsai. Plants with a woody stem in their second year are ideal candidates, and as with any other bonsai, you can use wire to help create a shape. Judicious pruning and positioning in the pot make the plant look more authentic. Never give bonsai fuchsia a high-nitrogen feed; a weak solution of a balanced feed is best. Keep the plants in a shady position to prevent them drying out. Gentle watering with a fine spray will gradually bring the top roots to the surface and expose them, and you can further enhance the bonsai effect by adding a little moss. Bonsai fuchsias can remain in the same container for many years.

SUITABLE FUCHSIAS TO GROW AS BONSAI

Where possible, try to look for plants with small flowers and a small growth habit, as they will look ideal as a bonsai. With their small leaves and delicate flowers, encliandras are good subjects, and so are the dwarf-growing hardies, such as Tom Thumb and Lady Thumb. Try foliage fuchsias as well. Always be prepared to experiment.

To achieve this sort of shape, bend wire gently around a young and supple stem.

A three-year-old Pumilla fuchsia.

David, an old, low-growing hardy, is an excellent choice.

1 *Remove as much soil and as many fibrous roots as possible from the plant you have chosen to train, so that it will fit comfortably into the shallow bonsai container.*

2 *If there are any larger roots that would be difficult to fit into a shallow pot, carefully trim these with secateurs. Do not worry – your plant will survive.*

3 *Choose the best position for planting your fuchsia in its pot. It need not be symmetrical, but should create a pleasing, bonsai-like appearance.*

4 *Gently trickle more soil into the tiny gaps around the roots of the plant. A small spoon is ideal for this. Do not press the soil down; it will find its own level.*

Put the moss gently in position. It will soon regrow.

5 *For a final bonsai touch, add a small piece of moss around the main stem. Put it in place and shape it as necessary. This piece came from the surface of an old fuchsia.*

6 *This is a good opportunity to trim branches and carry out any stopping required to shape the plant. To achieve an authentic bonsai shape, wire soft branches into 'windswept' positions.*

7 *Once you are happy with the plant, give it a little water and place it in a cool, shady spot. Leave it in this stress-free environment for up to a week and water it as necessary.*

FUCHSIAS IN NOVEL CONTAINERS

One of the great things about fuchsias – and what makes them so much fun to grow –
is that they are so adaptable and will grow in just about anything. Instead of
just sticking to conventional pots and baskets, why not be more adventurous
and try growing fuchsias in some novel containers?

Let your imagination run riot when considering the containers in which your fuchsias will look good growing and flowering. They do not have to be on a grand scale, but make sure they are in proportion to the size of the plant and the flowers. Small plants in small containers can be great fun. Look for containers with some kind of drainage. If there is none, then it may be possible to make holes in the base, but only if you do not want to use it for anything else afterwards! If drainage remains poor, water very carefully, giving your plants just the merest drop as necessary. A terracotta container with poor drainage is not such a problem as it is porous and water can seep

A watering can is an ideal container, provided you make plenty of drainage holes in the base. Do not put it in full sun for long, as the heat could cause the roots to scorch. Wassernymph (Waternymph) seems an ideal choice.

A small kettle with a large plant; this one is Superstar. Take care when planting around the handle. Gently manoeuvre the branches around it to achieve the desired effect.

A plant in a shoe is always a talking point. Push the potting mix very gently to the extremities, so that the roots can spread around. Olive Smith, a small, single-flowered cultivar, seems to be thriving.

Above: *Dancing Flame makes a fine display trailing over a terracotta cauldron. The plant can lose moisture through the porous pot, as well as via the drainage holes.*

POINTS TO WATCH

Take care when watering novelty containers, as many have poor drainage or none at all. Water them sparingly and do not forget to feed them. Try to find containers that are in proportion to the size of the flowers and growth habit of the plant; a small plant in a large pot (or vice-versa) can look very strange.

Below: *Drainage can be a major problem in a glazed pottery teapot with no holes. Water very carefully, giving only small quantities as and when the plant and potting mixture become dry.*

out of the sides, thus reducing the potential problems. Try matching fuchsia names with containers; for example, Trumpeter in a trumpet, Peppermint Stick in a sweet jar. Or why not match the size and shape of the plant to the style of the container? If possible, put the plant in your chosen container long before it is in flower so that the stress of the change does not cause it to drop flowers and buds. If it has to be a last-minute enterprise, keep the plant in a cool, shady spot for as long as possible to reduce the stress and allow it to recover from the change.

With its slightly trailing growth, Autumnale (Burning Bush), makes an ideal plant for this small display. As the plants are in ordinary pots on saucers it is easy to change the plants.

THE PROJECTS

A FUCHSIA FLOWER TOWER

Many fuchsias are natural and spectacular trailers, thus lending themselves perfectly to the economic modern container phenomenon that is the 'flower tower'. With a built-in reservoir, this is one of the most effective ways of getting the most from any fuchsia with a good trailing habit.

Today, the choice of containers for hanging displays is wider than ever. A recent development is a design based on a sturdy plastic bag. Follow the manufacturer's instructions for assembling a container like this; the one shown here has an integral drip tray that prevents splashing and also acts as a small extra water reservoir. Since the aim is to cover the sides of the tower as quickly as possible, always be sure to select fast-growing trailing plants with a dense branching habit and do not economise on the number of plants you buy. Trailing fuchsias such as 'La Campanella', 'Hula Girl' and 'Jack Shahan' are good choices. There is no need to buy large plants. Small 'plug' plants are ideal, since their tiny, narrow, pointed rootballs are easy to push in through the slits or crosses cut in the sides of the bag that are a feature of this growing medium. If only larger plants are available, carefully remove loose mix from the bases of their rootballs and tease out the roots to give a longer and narrower shape that is easier to get into the bag. Do

1 *Right: This hanging 'tower' has plastic sides and a solid drip tray base. Assemble and suspend it and add a layer of potting mix.*

Left: Here, the same variety of fuchsia has been used throughout the scheme. Although a dozen or more plants have been used to create the display, the effect is of one really big, outstanding fuchsia.

2 *Using a sharp pair of scissors, cut four or five crosses into the plastic just above the level of the potting mixture base, where you want to put plants. You will push the plants through the cuts, so ensure that they are big enough to take them. Prepare and plant only one layer at a time, working from the bottom up.*

3 *Tip small trailing fuchsias out of their pots, remove surplus soil from the roots and squeeze them gently into a narrow column that will fit through the crosses. Be careful not to damage the roots of the plant as you do this, and handle the plants gently as you squeeze their bases into shape.*

4 *Gently tuck the roots of the plants inside the bag so that they rest on the surface of the potting mix. Tuck the plastic back around the neck of the plant to stop the mix falling out and to help hold the plant in place.*

not cut off or break roots to fit, as this will damage the plants. Also, avoid making planting holes in the sides of the flower tower any larger than absolutely necessary, as potting mix tends to run out during watering.

As with normal hanging baskets, it is a good idea to add water-retaining gel crystals and slow-release fertiliser granules to the potting mix before planting the bag. This will help the plants to establish themselves. Check daily and water as often as needed.

If you take good care of your fuchsia flower tower, it should remain in good shape and give you months of pleasure.

5 *With the bottom row of plants in place, add another layer of potting mix to the tower. Do this slowly and evenly so that the wrinkles in the sides of the container are stretched out. Be careful to ensure that the plants in the bottom layer are not dislodged as you add more potting mix.*

6 ***Right:*** *Cut more crosses into the plastic halfway up the side walls, staggering them with the lower row of plants to create a more varied planting pattern on the outside of the container. Tuck the new plants in through the sides, in the same way as before.*

7 Put in a final row of plants as close as possible to the top of the container. Finish with a large single plant, which could be of a more upright type than the others.

8 Water evenly, so that the mix is moist but is not washed out through the planting holes. The drip tray prevents splashes and stops the tower from drying out too quickly.

9 **Right:** Keep the tower well watered, regularly fed and in a bright situation, but out of strong midday sun. After about six weeks, the plants will begin to cover the container and come into flower. Deadhead them often.

Left: Oxalis makes an unusual subject for this tower, but all sorts of fuchsias and other plants with plenty of small bright flowers and strikingly shaped contrasting dark foliage would work, too.

RAISING YOUR OWN FUCHSIA PLANTS

For a flower tower you will need a lot of plants of one cultivar for maximum effect; you can grow your own from cuttings. Start the small cuttings off early in the spring when they will root quickly and pot them on into small pots for a few weeks before planting so that they will be well rooted before they are moved on. Also, it will be much better if they have been stopped at least once before being left to grow on in the flower tower. For the first few weeks water carefully so that the plants have a chance to establish.

ALTERNATIVE FLOWER TOWER DISPLAYS

Right: As an alternative to fuchsias, trailing verbena makes a more traditional display. The dusky pink flowers contrast particularly well with the delicate ferny foliage. Look for plants with similar attributes for alternative schemes.

ASSORTED FUCHSIAS IN A BASKET

Many fuchsias combine well with one another and never look more spectacular than when they are sympathetically arranged in an attractive basket. However, it is important to use varieties with similar growing habits and flowering times, as otherwise the basket can quickly become a jumbled mess.

The fuchsias used here are all quite similar types, with medium to small flowers, both single and double. Basket types are suitable, as well as upright-growing kinds. Cut them from large plants and leave the foliage intact to provide colour contrast and definition. It would be an ideal way to display branches of hardy types that you have picked from the garden and brought indoors. Treat the stems of fuchsias as you would any other cut flower material. Split woody stems a little to allow better absorption of water and cut green stems at an angle neatly and cleanly. You could adapt this idea and create it using a basket made from other material, although the moss is an important part of the design and should be clearly visible through the sides of the container.

1 *Start by lining the wire basket with fresh, damp moss. You will find it easier to work using several small pieces.*

2 *Push the pieces of moss against the sides of the basket and as far up as possible while the basket remains empty.*

3 *Now line the basket with a piece of thin black plastic cut roughly to shape.*

4 *Cut a block of damp flower foam to fit inside the basket, stopping just below the top.*

5 *Start to push the fuchsia stems into the foam. The aim is to create a good all-round effect.*

6 *Continue building up the arrangement, adding more stems to make a fairly dense mixture. Let one or two stems drop down low at the front and sides of the basket.*

Pacquesa

Snowcap

Dollar Princess

Mary

Rufus

Margaret Brown

7 *Stand the finished basket either at table height or a little higher to appreciate the hanging fuchsia flowers better. Spray the flowers occasionally with a fine mist of water to keep the basket fresh and vigorous.*

89

FUCHSIAS IN A MIXED BASKET

One effective method of growing fuchsias is to combine them with other plants, including the small 'cell' plants now widely available and known as 'plugs'. These can be purchased by mail order or easily acquired from garden centres. There are countless different varieties, many of which will work well with fuchsias.

So far in this book we have concentrated mainly on fuchsias on their own in containers, but for many people the best way of growing fuchsias is in a mixed basket with a range of other trailing plants; some may be flowering plants, others mainly for foliage, so that you truly get the best of both worlds. There are so many different plants available today that you can really experiment. Find out which plants do best in a hot spot – if that is where your baskets hang. If your baskets are positioned in a shady corner, then choose plants that will thrive in a cooler area.

You can also take advantage of the wide range of 'plug' plants from early spring onwards. 'Plugs' are young plants grown in

1 *Assemble a mixture of flowering and foliage plants, with trailing varieties to cover the basket sides and bushy, upright types for the middle.*

Left: In this sumptuous hanging basket, a fuchsia predominates yet at the same time ties in beautifully with petunias and pelargoniums. The versatility of fuchsias is nowhere more apparent than in hanging baskets.

2 *Place a circle of black plastic in the bottom of the basket to act as a water reservoir. Add some potting mixture to hold it in place.*

small individual 'cells', rather like multiple egg boxes on a tiny scale. Remove each plantlet from its cell before planting, by pushing the tip of a dibber or pencil carefully up through the base of the cell. Plugs make planting very simple; root damage is virtually non-existent, as the plugs can simply be pushed into loose potting mix. They are particularly easy to use around the sides of fuchsia hanging baskets, as they are small enough to fit through the wire sides of traditional baskets.

Select a number of plants for your basket, ideally in pairs or threes so that you can build up a symmetrical planting, and then let your imagination run wild! The photographs on this page show a moss lined basket, which is very much the traditional way of lining a basket, but look out for other forms of liners that are now available – holes can be made in them for your plants to slot through. The advantage of these basket liners is that they can reduce the water loss from your basket and make watering easier. Choose the type of liner that suits you best.

Once your basket is planted, don't forget to give it a good water and then leave it somewhere frost free until the time has come to put it outside. The earlier in the year that you can plant up a basket the better it will be, as the plant will have had time to establish before you put it outside for the summer.

3 *Tuck a layer of sphagnum moss under the edge of the plastic. Once the basket is full, you will not notice the plastic at all.*

91

4 *Build up the sides with a thick layer of moss. Pack it in tightly to prevent soil escaping when the plants are watered. Add more potting mix on top.*

5 *Gently push the neck of the plant just inside the wire. Pack it with moss and cover the rootball with more mix, filling in any gaps.*

6 *Plant the ivy, holding the rootball horizontally and feeding the trails through the wires from inside out. Push the crown against the inside of the basket. When the sides are planted up, cover all the exposed rootballs with more mix. Leave space for planting in the top. Add more trailing plants to hang over the top of the basket. Fill in the centre with upright plants; leave room for growth.*

7 *Left: Cover the surface with a thick layer of moss. Water the basket well and hang it in a light, frost-free place until the plants are established. Once young plants develop a good root system, they quickly fill the basket. Feed regularly to keep them flowering.*

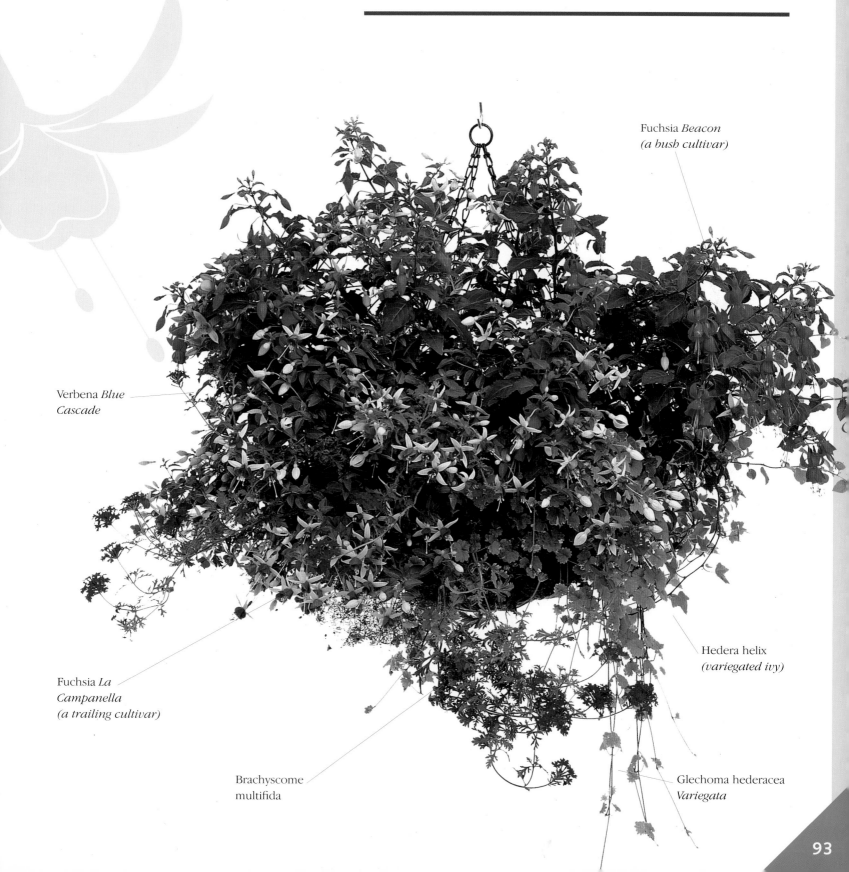

Fuchsia *Beacon*
(a bush cultivar)

Verbena *Blue*
Cascade

Hedera helix
(variegated ivy)

Fuchsia *La*
Campanella
(a trailing cultivar)

Brachyscome
multifida

Glechoma hederacea
Variegata

HELP!

SUMMER CARE

Once fuchsias are in flower there is a tendency to neglect them, but this is just the time
that they need your closest attention. Feeding is particularly important
during the summer, as providing a balanced feed once a week will promote
continual flowering over a long period.

Carry out regular maintenance once a week in the summer – more frequently if possible – to ensure that your plants continue to flower for many months. Take off all the seedpods, dead flowers and yellow leaves and check generally that there are no problems with the plants. Vigilance and care during the summer months will ensure that you always spot any problems caused by pests or diseases at an early stage.

BEES' FOOTPRINTS

Insects visiting flowers to collect nectar may gradually damage the petals. Examine the flowers closely and you may find small, dark patches on them. If you wish to show your plants, move them to a place where the insects cannot reach them.

Watering is vital at this time of year, otherwise fuchsias will lose their leaves and flowers. However, do not overwater; check the dampness of the soil by feeling the surface with your fingers. It should only ever be damp to the touch, never soggy. In the hottest weather, fuchsias may need watering several times each day. If it remains hot for prolonged periods, it could be worth installing a drip-feed watering system that supplies a trickle of water to each plant through a network of small-bore tubes laid on the ground. Plenty of shade should reduce the need for watering.

Left: *When fuchsias are planted in a garden border, nature will take care of most of the tidying and maintenance tasks for you. Wind and rain will knock the old flowers off the stems. Water border fuchsias regularly, as they have not had time to establish a full root run. Feed them several times during the growing season.*

Right: *Remove any seedpods that remain after the flowers have gone. If they have been fertilized and are allowed to develop into mature fruits, the plant is less likely to continue flowering.*

Below: *Tubs require more care in summer. Remove dead blooms, seedpods and yellow leaves every week to ensure the longest possible flowering period. Feed the tubs once a week in summer. When feeding and watering, take care not to get liquid on the leaves, as this can cause scorching.*

Below: *Fuchsia flowers that are almost dead come away easily if you pull them gently. In some cultivars, dead flowers fall off readily, while in others they hang on until removed.*

Above: *Remove yellowing, dead or damaged leaves to improve the general appearance of the plant. At the same time, examine the plant for any signs of pests and diseases.*

PRUNING BASKET FUCHSIAS

As we have seen, fuchsias are wonderful plants for hanging baskets, but they will lose their shape quite quickly if they are not properly tended to and given a regular pruning. Not only will pruning help to restore the fuchsia's looks – it will keep the plant healthier and generally happier, too.

As fuchsias approach the end of their growing and flowering season, the foliage starts to turn yellow and there are few new flowers. This is the time to give them a rest and to create a plant with a good shape and structure for the following year. Never be afraid to cut back a plant. Baskets and standards will do better the following year if you have cut them back carefully. Shape the

plants as you cut until you are happy with the woody structure. Strip away any leaves that remain on the stems and remove any debris on the surface of the soil. Remove the plant from its pot and check that no vine weevils are present. Examine the roots for evidence of chewing, patches of missing roots and holes in the soil. If you find any of these, excavate gently with your fingers until you

2 *Aim to create a sound structure for the following year, but retain a sufficient amount of growth so that any possible die back in the winter will not endanger the final shape of the plant the next season.*

1 *At the end of the growing and flowering season, hanging baskets lose all inclination to flower. Cutting them back at this time will force them into a period of rest. Any subsequent new growth will be fresh and full of vigour.*

When dealing with round-bottomed baskets, sit them in a bucket to stop them rolling around.

3 *Leave the main branches long enough so that they are already beginning to hang over the edge, ready for next season. Use sharp secateurs so that you cut rather than tear the stems.*

4 *You can see the finished effect and even make out the shape if it is unbalanced. Label all the plants, as it is easy to forget which is which when they resume growing in the spring.*

5 *Remove any leaves that remain on the stems. Clear away debris on the surface of the potting mixture to prevent the development of problems with mould, etc., during the winter months.*

find the vine weevil larvae and remove them. Label your plants while you can still remember what they are or just make a note of the colours. If you leave the fuchsia in the same potting mixture during the winter, and do not disturb the rootball, either repot it into the same basket in spring or leave it as a second-year basket in the same soil. Add a little fresh potting mixture on the surface and feed plants regularly.

Shortly after cutting, the stems may bleed a little with a clear liquid. This will soon stop and does not harm the plant.

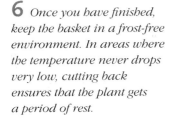

6 *Once you have finished, keep the basket in a frost-free environment. In areas where the temperature never drops very low, cutting back ensures that the plant gets a period of rest.*

CUTTING BACK A STANDARD FUCHSIA

At the end of a growing season we come to one of the most important jobs of the year: pruning back a standard. With a bit of care and a steady hand we can make a good standard even better. Be brave, and prune away to your heart's content – it will pay dividends over the years!

Patience, a medium-sized double with white-flushed, pale pink flowers.

When a fuchsia still has a few buds and green leaves left on it, it is very tempting to hesitate about cutting it back. However, failure to cut back will mean that over a period of time, the standard will deteriorate. The head will grow larger and larger, but the flowers and growth will become more and more sparse. With good care and an annual cut back, standard fuchsias can survive for many years – a heavily pruned standard has been known to

1 *At the end of the season, fuchsias start to look tired, with yellow leaves and a clear lack of flower. This is an ideal time to give the plant a good rest and prune it back thoroughly.*

2 *When pruning a standard fuchsia, the aim is to produce a good, woody shape and structure for the new growth. Use a sharp pair of secateurs.*

3 *Work your way around the plant to create a pleasing and well-balanced shape.*

Try to cut above a division of branches to maintain a more substantial structure.

Do not cut off any more growth on this side.

4 *As you prune more of the old growth of the plant away, the shape of the existing woody structure becomes clearer. This is a good opportunity to make a lop-sided plant more symmetrical and generally better-looking.*

5 *It is amazing how much you will cut away as you work, and how much of the plant you can see. Ideally, the head should be no more than a third to a half of its original size when you have finished.*

live as long as 20 years. As you cut back the standard, it is important to visualize the final shape that you are aiming to achieve. By careful cutting you should be able to create a woody structure that is at the very least as good as the current year's growth. With careful trimming, you should be able to create an even better woody shape that will pay dividends in the following growing season. Where possible, cut above a fork in the branches, so that as many branches as possible will develop. If you prune in warm

conditions, there is little delay between cutting back and the appearance of new growth. Within 10 to 14 days, small specks of new growth will start to sprout. The speed at which they develop will depend on the climate. In temperatures of over 10°C (50°F), fuchsias continue to grow and you will soon see a fine new head on a standard.

6 *Once you have finished cutting, remove all the leaves left on the wood, otherwise you may encounter problems with fungal infections, such as botrytis and damping-off.*

7 *Now there is a good framework for the new growth in the following season. There may be a little leakage of sap, but this will soon stop and does not harm the plant.*

PREPARING YOUR FUCHSIAS FOR WINTER

How you prepare fuchsias for the winter depends very much on the severity
of the weather in your area. If frosts are extremely rare, you need
not take many precautions, but your plants will still need a dormant period,
otherwise they become weak and will not give you the best results.

Cut back your plants as described on pages 98–99. They will continue to grow unless a cold spell occurs and checks their development, in which case you may find it useful to keep some lightweight fleece to hand for added protection. Fleece is available from nurseries and garden centres.

Assuming you live in an area with a relatively harsh winter and a number of frosts, these are the precautions you should take. Once a plant has been prepared, move it to a heated greenhouse or an alternative frost-free environment. If it is kept below freezing point for more than a short time, a plant will die.

At 0–4°C (32–39°F) the plant will survive and not grow. Above this temperature the plant will resume growing. Never let your plants dry out entirely during the winter; always check that the soil is damp.

1 *Plants that are coming to the end of their growing season start to look tired and have yellow leaves. They need to rest in winter; cutting back forces them to stop growing.*

2 *The aim of cutting back is to produce a good structure of woody stems, half the size of the original plant. Now is the time to correct any defects that have appeared in the shape of the plant.*

Use a good sharp pair of secateurs to enable you to make clean cuts into the wood rather than tearing it, which could encourage disease.

3 *The more wood you remove, the clearer the structure that you are aiming for will become. Remove the largest branches first, to get to the centre of the plant which defines its shape.*

4 *Once the largest branches have been cut back, you can look at the smaller branches that remain and then cut them to create the shape that you want.*

5 *When you have achieved the desired shape, remove any leaves left on the stems and clean away any debris on the surface of the pot to prevent botrytis and damping-off.*

The fleece allows the light through, so plants will grow underneath without being damaged.

Right: *In an area that is almost frost-free, lightweight fleece will give the plants a little extra protection. A single layer will give protection to −1.5°C (29°F), a double layer will give several more degrees of protection.*

Above: *A cardboard box filled with polystyrene foam chips is excellent insulation and allows the plant to survive the winter. Surround the plant to keep it as warm as possible.*

PRUNING HARDY FUCHSIAS

All hardy fuchsias require pruning at some stage, even if you live in an area with few or no frosts, otherwise they become tired. When you prune them depends very much on the local climate, because you must wait until there is no danger of frost that could damage the young growth.

If you are in any doubt about the climate in your area and whether the danger of frost has passed, delay pruning your fuchsias, because they really will not thank you if the young growth is subjected to a late attack of cold weather. In areas where frosts occur, plants will die back to ground level. However, once you are certain it is safe to proceed, attack with enthusiasm!

If the plant has died back as a result of a late frost, you must wait until the new growth has reached 5–7.5cm (2–3in) high before you consider cutting off the dead wood. Where a plant is slightly damaged by the colder weather but new growth appears part of the way up the stems, adopt a more cautious pruning method. When you cut back these plants, think along the lines of cutting back a bush and aim to create a good shape for the new growth. Carry out a less enthusiastic but firm cut just above the new growth.

1 *It is important to remove the old wood that has been killed by the frosts. Use sharp secateurs to make clean cuts. Work carefully, so that there is no risk of damaging the new young shoots.*

Cut low into the old wood so that it does not look unsightly.

Left: *If they have been caught by the frosts, hardy fuchsias will need pruning in the spring to remove the dead wood. In areas without frosts, fuchsias will still need partial pruning to ensure that they give a good show.*

Dorothy, a hardy with beautiful bell-shaped flowers. It makes a low-growing mound about 60cm (24in) high.

2 *Gradually remove the dead wood, cutting each stem until it is 5–7.5cm (2–3in) above ground level. Doing this after the new growth has appeared allows you to see clearly what has been affected by the cold weather.*

3 *As you remove the last stem you can see that a new bushy plant is emerging with fine healthy growth. A little feed at this stage will give the plant a good start.*

However, if you do not want the plant to get too large, cut it back more firmly than you usually would. Finally, in areas where frosts never or rarely occur and the plant has no reason to die back at all, it is still a good idea to prune hardy fuchsias once a year. Prune the whole plant in one go or, if you prefer a less drastic method, carefully prune one third of the branches and another third of them later in the year.

Left: *Cardinal Farges is a bright, hardy fuchsia, originally from France. The flowers are semi-double and it has a compact growth habit. As with all fuchsias, pruning encourages it to produce healthy, new growth.*

Young healthy growth on Pixie, which has light foliage and rose and light mauve flowers

4 *The fuchsia will return to its original size within weeks. This growing method means that you need not worry about turning or stopping - nature will create healthy, bushy plants.*

HINTS ON PRUNING

Never cut fuchsias back before the frosts have ended; leaving the dead twigs on the plant will help to protect against the frost and increases the plant's chances of survival during the coldest months.

Earthing up the crown of the plant with soil or leaves also helps. Start cutting back only when the danger of hard frosts in your area has passed and when the new growth is showing strongly.

If the plants have not been killed right back, prune off only the dead wood, leaving the new growth intact to give the plant a greater size than before.

ROOT TRIMMING A FUCHSIA

During the growing season there can come a time when you feel that the plant needs a little fresh compost, but cannot go up into a larger pot. This is when root trimming offers the best solution. Don't be afraid to perform this technique; it may seem a little drastic, but as you will see the results are incredible!

Left: To keep a plant such as this in full flower for the whole summer, you may need to take decisive action! Lucinda, a fine semi-double, will flower profusely in good conditions.

There will be times during the growing season when you would like to keep a plant in the same size pot, but the plant has become potbound and the foliage is beginning to look stale.

This is a time for drastic action! If you remove about 2.5cm (1in) from the base of the rootball with a knife or small saw, and put the plant back into the same pot, you will achieve two things. Firstly, you will refresh the plant by giving it a new root run; after a small check, the plant will again grow briskly with fresh and healthy growth. Secondly, you will be able to drop the plant slightly lower in the pot, which will allow you to put some fresh potting mix on top and cover up areas of bare stems where the lower leaves have dropped off.

If the plant will not drop lower in the pot, shave a little off the sides of the rootball so that it will fit snugly. The fresh potting mix on the top will also promote healthy growth, as the feeding roots are found there. This fresh layer of soil will soon be full of roots and the plant will race ahead of those that have not received this treatment.

1 *This Waveney Gem has been in the same pot for many months. Its roots are beginning to circle the pot – a sign that it is becoming potbound.*

2 *Begin to cut the base of the rootball. Never carry out this action when the plant is in full flower: it is too much of a shock.*

3 *Cut a clean slice about 2.5cm (1in) across the base of the rootball, and off the sides if necessary, and gently remove it. Do not be afraid to tackle this procedure, as fuchsias replace their roots very quickly. With a large, old plant it may need doing every year. If the plant has particularly large or tough roots, you may need to use a saw as opposed to the knife illustrated here.*

4 *Add an equivalent amount of fresh soil to the base of the pot. It is better to use too much than to leave an air gap, which is not good for the plant.*

5 *Lower the plant into the pot. It should fit comfortably and rest gently on the fresh soil.*

6 *Press down lightly on the rootball to remove any air spaces and add a little more fresh soil over the surface of the existing rootball. Water the plant gently to settle the soil.*

Left: *Four weeks after this apparently drastic treatment, Waveney Gem is now full of flower.*

107

PESTS AND DISEASES

Luckily, fuchsias do not suffer from too many pests and diseases,
but it is worth familiarizing yourself with potential problems so that you will
know what to look for. If a particular problem is not covered here,
consult your local nursery; they will be happy to help you.

Whitefly is probably the most common problem wherever you grow fuchsias. Whiteflies are all female and can produce subsequent generations at incredible speed. Over the years, they have become resistant to most sprays, but *Encarsia formosa*, a minute predatory type of wasp, is very efficient at eliminating them under glass.

Aphids, particularly greenfly, are very much a seasonal problem. Left to multiply, they will gradually distort young growth on the plant. A number of chemical sprays are available and these will normally solve the problem. There is also a predator, *Aphidius matricariae*, but it is relatively large and mobile and, unless your plants are in an enclosed area, it is likely to fly away.

Red spider mites are more of a problem, as they are so small that most people do not see the pests, just the damage that they cause. The first signs of the mite are small white dots on the upper surface of the leaf, but again they are extremely difficult to see. Tackle the problem either with sprays or a natural predator, *Phytoseiulus persimilius*. Also remove and destroy any damaged leaves and isolate affected plants. Red spider mite tends to thrive in a dry environment, so promote humid conditions to discourage it.

Although adult vine weevils do not cause fuchsias too much damage, their larvae can create serious problems and you should check your plants regularly for signs of their presence.

Above: A single aphid. These insects multiply rapidly. They suck out the contents of leaf cells, causing damage to immature leaves and growing tips.

Left: This plant is suffering from a particularly heavy infestation of red spider mite. Even the tops of the leaves are affected. They are turning brown and beginning to roll under.

Right: All the stages of the whitefly problem on one leaf. The adults are attracted to yellow.

Above: Rust occurs in warm, poorly ventilated conditions. The spores on the leaves are easily dislodged and transferred from plant to plant.

A mature whitefly resembles a tiny white moth, less than 1mm (0.04in) long.

Here, the parasitic wasps, Encarsia, *have laid their eggs within the whitefly scales.*

Scales contain the immature whitefly.

Above: You can see the small red spider mites and webbing on the underside of the leaf. They pierce the leaves and suck out the contents of the cells, causing discolouration.

Right: The only way to treat a plant which is badly infected by red spider mites is to cut it hard back and burn the plant material. Water the potting mixture with an appropriate chemical to destroy any remaining mites.

Above: *Treating a plant with vine weevil nematode worm solution. This is the most effective way to deal with vine weevils once they have established themselves.*

Rust is a fungus problem that will never kill a plant, but can cause severe problems if it is left unchecked. The fungus is found within the system of the plant and will produce areas of fruiting bodies that produce vast quantities of spores on the underside of leaves. It thrives where plants are kept close together and the ventilation is poor, so improving these conditions will reduce the chance of rust taking a hold on your plants. Remove and destroy any damaged leaves from affected plants and, if the problem is severe, do the same with the top layer of soil. Spraying regularly with a fungicide will control the problem.

If you decide to use sprays to keep pests and diseases at bay, always follow the manufacturer's instructions carefully and be sure to take any necessary precautions. Never mix sprays or increase the dose. If in doubt, ask for advice.

Finally, here are some useful tips which should hopefully reduce the chances of your plants falling prey to pests and diseases:

• Keep a close watch on your plants and catch any possible problem before it takes hold; remember, preventing a problem is always better than trying to cure it.

• If you are using any sprays always follow all the instructions – they are there for a good reason.

• Whitefly in particular can become resistant to sprays – use several different ones in

Below: *Botrytis or grey leaf mould can be a problem for fuchsias, as it is for many plants. It can attack leaves, stems and flowers and is particularly likely to occur in wet conditions, showing as a fluffy, grey mould. Remove the offending part and spray with carbendazim as soon as you see the first signs of attack on your plants.*

rotation so that they are less likely to become resistant.

• If you spot a few whitefly early in the year, don't wait until the problem becomes worse: gently squash them with your thumb and finger, being careful not to damage the leaf.

• During the summer months, to reduce a potential problem of red spider keep the area around the plants humid; spray the floor or ground regularly with water to maintain an ideal environment.

• In the winter, too much damp in the atmosphere can produce problems with rust, botrytis or damping off, so keep air moving around the plants to reduce the chance of this problem occurring. Maintain a gap between plants so that problems are less likely to spread.

• Be vigilant, chewed 'U' shapes out of leaves means that potentially adult vine weevil are around; have a look under the foliage and pot – you may spot one in a darker spot. If not, take a close look after dark.

• Repotting plants in the autumn is your best chance of catching vine weevil before they do too much damage. Replace outer compost with fresh compost, or if the damage is bad, remove all compost and replace it with fresh compost.

• Look out for new products that are available to control vine weevil and can be watered into compost – they do work.

Left: Cuckoo spit is not a major problem for fuchsias, but it is unsightly and the white, frothy mass houses the larvae of the froghopper, which could damage the plants if left untended for long enough. If you see cuckoo spit on your fuchsias, either pick it off by hand or dislodge it with a jet of water to wash away the young froghoppers inside.

VINE WEEVILS

Vine weevil larvae (shown bottom right) will kill fuchsias if not controlled. The adults (shown below) are a minor problem, as they only chew the edges of leaves, leaving small horseshoe-shaped indentations. Being nocturnal, they are not easy to spot, but if you find one, tread on it! Vine weevils are all female and lay their eggs in the top of the soil during the summer months. These hatch and become larvae, with the sole aim of eating roots (not only fuchsia roots but those of many other types of plant as well). In the autumn, you can often spot early signs of damage by taking the plant out of its pot and examining it for chewed and brown roots.

Look in the area of damage and you will find the larvae; remove them and feed them to the birds! Alternatively, control them biologically, using a nematode worm called *Heterorhabditis sp.*

HYBRIDIZING FUCHSIAS

There can be nothing more fascinating than the prospect of producing a brand new cultivar by crossing different fuchsias. However, be warned; there are approximately 10,000 fuchsia varieties around the world, so the chances of producing something entirely different are fairly small!

The photographs on these pages clearly show how to carry out the fertilization process. Once the seedpods have matured and are looking like little grapes, remove them carefully from the plant. Cut each fruit open and you will see a central area surrounded by a mass of small seeds. Detach these using a cocktail stick or similar implement and tip them onto an absorbent surface. Viable seeds are larger than the rest and often darker – they will also sink when placed in water. Dry the seeds and keep them safe and carefully labeled. Plant the seeds at the normal time and in the usual way. Be patient, as some may take quite a while to germinate. Do not throw away the potting mixture for several months as something special may still appear! Grow the plants as you would any other fuchsia. Waiting for those first flowers to open can be quite an experience! Keep a note of the cultivars used and the date, particularly if you do a number of crosses between the same or

Twist ties are fine for sealing the bag, provided you use them carefully.

Pop open an almost mature bud by gently squeezing it so that nothing is damaged inside.

1 *Choose a cultivar with characteristics that you like and prepare it to become the female partner in the pollination process. Selecting a young bud is vital so that you can isolate the female parts before they become mature and open to pollination.*

2 *Use scissors to cut away all the anthers and filaments (the male parts of the flower). This will prevent the flower pollinating itself. Be careful not to damage the flower – hold it gently between your fingers and ensure that the blades of your scissors are as sharp as possible.*

3 ***Above:*** *Gently enclose the emasculated flower in a plastic bag. This will allow you to see the flower as it matures, but also to give the flower protection from being pollinated by another fuchsia.*

Fuchsias have eight stamens and they must all be removed. At this early stage they can be well hidden in the petals, so hunt around if they are not immediately apparent.

different cultivars. Take cuttings of any plant you consider good enough to keep and nurture them for another three years to ensure that the cultivar holds all its characteristics. Your local specialist nursery or fuchsia society will advise you if it is worth continuing with your new cultivar plant.

4 *Test the maturity of the flower by placing your finger gently on the tip of the stigma – if slightly sticky then it is receptive. To make the rest of the procedure easier, you can remove the petals if you wish.*

5 *Carefully remove the pistil (female parts) from the flower chosen to be the male one. Test for ripe pollen by brushing your finger over it – ripe pollen grains will stick to your finger.*

6 **Left:** *With both flowers ready, remove the plastic bag from around the female flower and bring the male flower to it so that the pollen grains can be accepted by the stigma.*

You can remove the bag once the flower has fallen off, leaving the seedpod.

Gently brush the two flowers together.

7 **Above:** *After the pollination process, isolate the flower again to avert random pollination if your attempt has failed. Use a plastic or muslin bag to protect the flower while the seedpods develop at the base.*

A young pair of seedpods. Fuchsias have either green or reddish purple pods at maturity – which can take several weeks.

8 *It is possible that the seedpods (berries) may fall off at an early stage, indicating that fertilization was not successful. Therefore, it is worth doing several flowers at the same time to increase your chances of success.*

GROWING FUCHSIAS INDOORS

Seeing a lovely fuchsia in full flower during the summer often seems an invitation to bring it indoors to enjoy. However, unless a plant has acclimatised to life in the dry atmosphere of a house, the flowers and leaves will fall in a matter of days. Follow the tips below and you will be able to enjoy your plants in the house.

1 *Choose a plant that is not in flower. Put some small pebbles into a large saucer. This will raise the plant above the eventual water level so that it does not become waterlogged.*

2 *Add some water to the saucer, taking care that the level does not rise above the pebbles. The plant should not sit directly in water for long periods of time.*

GOOD FUCHSIAS FOR INDOORS

Baby Chang;
Bambini;
Chang;
Dollar Princess;
Heidi Ann;
Leonora;
Little Beauty;
Little Jewel;
Minirose;
Nellie Nuttall;
Saturnus;
Sandboy;
Tom West.

Fuchsias do not always make ideal houseplants, but given a little extra care and attention they will thrive. Fuchsias need a humid microclimate all around them, so spray them every day if possible, but be careful of the furniture!

As an additional precaution to keep your plants healthy and happy, you should also take them once a week to an area where you can mist them thoroughly to clean them and remove dust and grime from the leaf surfaces. Never place fuchsias too close to direct sunlight or to a source of heat, such as a radiator or electric fire. Make sure that the plants are not stressed, particularly if they are in flower or bud. Stress at such a time will cause them to lose both buds and flowers. If possible, start growing the fuchsia indoors as

Purpur Klokje is a cultivar from Holland. It has small claret and burgundy flowers.

The smaller plants shown below are less mature. As they develop, they will acclimatize and should not suffer from bud drop, which can result from a sudden change in environment. Plants with small flowers do well indoors.

Upward Look is a small-flowered single, with flowers that point upwards.

Heidi Ann

a small cutting and keep it inside so that it becomes accustomed to the environment. This is safer than expecting an outdoor plant to adjust to a sudden change. Feeding and general care are just as important for plants living indoors, as is vigilance regarding pests and diseases. Turning is perhaps even more important indoors, as the light will be coming only from one direction – that is, from the nearest window or door. Give the plant a quarter turn once a day to achieve the best all-round appearance. With care and attention, it is possible to grow any fuchsia indoors, but it is a good idea to concentrate on short-jointed and compact plants, as the others tend to become straggly and rather unwieldy when grown indoors.

3 Put the plant onto the pebbles. Water evaporating from the surface of the pebbles will provide a humid microclimate for the plant. It might not seem as though such a small measure would make much difference to the plant, but you would be surprised.

4 Regular, daily gentle spraying also helps to increase humidity. A more thorough spray once a week will clean the leaves and helps the plant to survive in the artificial environment.

SHOWING FUCHSIAS

Once you have grown a plant of which you are justifiably proud, you may well feel
that the time has come to show it to everyone else! Most specialist
societies have an annual show or display that could
provide you with just the opportunity.

Taking part in a fuchsia show, whether it is competitive or not, is great fun and allows you to meet other fuchsia enthusiasts in a friendly atmosphere. Additionally, the organizers are always keen to have as many plants as possible to make the occasion a spectacle, so you will always be made to feel welcome.

Any plant that you consider taking along to a show must be pest- and disease-free and have a good, healthy appearance. Ideally, the plants should be symmetrical and full of flower, the flowers being typical for the cultivar. There will be opportunities to include most types of fuchsias, and often there is an area where individual blooms are exhibited, either for artistic effect in a shallow dish, in sand or in small containers for six or twelve blooms. Each bloom should be as perfect as you can find, typical in shape, size and colour and with no markings on it. The anther and filaments and the stigma and style should all be fully extended. Pollen should just about be showing on the anthers. Get all these factors together and you will have the perfect flower!

1 *Remove any damaged or marked blooms from the plant. These show up clearly on a light-coloured plant such as this one, but on a dark-coloured fuchsia, look for flowers with brown or discoloured areas.*

2 *Remove the green seedpods right back to the main stem, as any small pieces of stalk will detract from the final effect.*

116

3 *Search carefully for any yellow leaves and remove them. Also remove debris, such as leaves and dead flowers, from the potting mixture.*

4 *Show plants need to be as symmetrical as possible and often need a final tie-in just before the show. If the plant has a lax growth, consider tying it in at the time of the last stop.*

5 *Insert three canes into the potting mixture in a triangular pattern around the edge of the pot. With a particularly large plant, you may need to use four canes.*

6 *Draw a string between the canes, bringing the plant in to create a good shape. Tie any loose branches separately to a cane or to another branch. The string should not be seen.*

7 *Using sharp secateurs, cut off any protruding pieces of cane, so that they are below the level of the majority of the growth. Do not cut the plant!*

8 *Once you are happy that the plant looks its best, wipe the pot with a damp cloth. Position the plant with its best side facing forward and leave the rest to the judges!*

Olive Moon ready for the show. This type of clearing up will help the plant to continue in flower for many months.

117

VARIETY GUIDE

FUCHSIA

ANITA

FUCHSIA

AUTUMNALE

FUCHSIA

BELLA ROSELLA

No collection of fuchsias should be without some vivid orange flowers, as they will brighten up any spot in your garden or on your patio. Anita is a small but floriferous single; the tube and sepals are brilliant white and the petals an incredibly vivid orange. The foliage is a dark shade of green with just a hint of bronze. Anita will be among the first to flower, and with regular feed and water will give many months of delightful flowers. The hybridizer of this wonderful little fuchsia has produced many excellent fuchsias, all showing similar characteristics of being easy to grow and producing lots of flowers. Other examples include Lambada and Daniella. My favourite way of growing Anita is as a standard, but grow it as a bush or in the garden and either way it will be very rewarding.

Also known as Burning Bush, this is a fuchsia that really lives up to its names! Autumnale has been grown for its beautiful foliage for more than 120 years. It features incredibly strong autumnal colours – with shades of red, orange, yellow and green all vying for attention. Autumnale has a distinctive style of growth – neither truly trailing nor upright, but more horizontal in style. Grow Autumnale in a light spot to get the best coloured foliage. The flowers are single, the tube and sepals rich red and the petals purple. Autumnale is a highly adaptable fuchsia which can be grown as a bush or in a basket – either on its own or as a brilliant splash of colour before other basket plants flower. If you like a challenge, Autumnale as a standard will take your breath away.

This cultivar has some of the largest flowers that I know, and it is also a great fuchsia to grow as it is so quick to develop, producing an abundance of enormous flowers. The superb blooms have tube and sepals of pale whitish pink; frills of petals are rich mauve with magenta edging. The weight of the flowers means that this plant is ideal both for baskets and pots. In a pot it can need a little staking and tying so that the weight of the flowers can be supported. Bella Rosella was bred from a cross of two great fuchsias, Quasar and Applause, both of which have large flowers. However, Bella Rosella probably exceeds them both in terms of the size of its flowers!

FUCHSIA

BEN DE JONG

FUCHSIA

CHECKERBOARD

FUCHSIA

DANCING FLAME

This fuchsia is one of the most delightful Triphylla type fuchsias. The flowers come in small clusters of three or four flowers. The tube is a rich rose, the sepals are tipped green and the petals are brightest orange. Like all Triphylla types, it will thrive in a hot and sunny spot and will give you many months of pleasure. Ben de Jong is another highly adaptable fuchsia which looks good in pots and tubs, planted as summer bedding (Triphyllas are not frost lovers), or grown it into a truly spectacular standard. Ben de Jong is a fast grower and will fill up a pot very quickly. Do not forget that hot colours look great in the garden and will brighten up a dull spot on your patio.

If I was limited to the number of different fuchsias that I could grow, however few that number might be Checkerboard would always be on my list. Checkerboard is an elegant single with long tubed flowers of red, the sepals are white and the petals are dark red. It is a really strong grower, with long arching branches dripping with flowers. Checkerboard will flower right throughout the summer, often being amongst the last to stop flowering. It is as a standard that Checkerboard excels, and after several years the head will often measure as much as 1–1.2m (3–4ft) across. My other favourite way to grow Checkerboard is in a large container, because this way once again you can appreciate the elegance of its flowers and growth. This fuchsia is a must for any collection.

Stubbs, 1981. Annabel Stubbs, a great American hybridizer of fuchsias, has over the years produced a number of fuchsias that are probably to be found in most keen fuchsia growers' collections. Good examples are Applause and Pink Marshmallow. Annabel's trademark is large luscious doubles, and Dancing Flame is no exception. The tube and sepals are light orange, and the petals are dark orange, with the occasional splash of vivid pink. Dancing Flame is a fuchsia that will look great in a hanging basket or tub. Although its flowers are large, Dancing Flame will produce an incredible mass of them throughout the summer months.

FUCHSIA

DARK EYES

FUCHSIA

DELTA'S GROOM

FUCHSIA

F. FULGENS RUBRA GRANDIFLORA

Erickson, 1958. This is probably one of the most adaptable fuchsias that I have ever grown: it can look great in a basket; it is superb in a tub; it can be really quite hardy; it excels as a standard – need I say more? It is not a new fuchsia and has stood the test of time really well – indeed, there is nothing more modern that comes anywhere near this variety. The flowers are double and really firm, with lots of petals. The tube and sepals are deep red, the petals are deep violet blue, and they fade to a deep lilac as the flower matures. The foliage is a dark green with a distinctive glossy sheen.

The aubergine or dark burgundy coloured fuchsias make a welcome change from the normal colour range of fuchsias and this is one of the best – a really strong grower, with large bell-shaped single flowers. The tube and sepals are light aubergine and the petals a darker shade. The Delta type fuchsias come in many shapes and sizes but this – along with its all-white partner Delta's Bride – is one of the best that I have grown. Delta's Bride has petals that fold right back like a saucer.

Any fuchsia from the aubergine range of colours will create a stir wherever it is seen. These varieties open our eyes to a whole new range of fuchsias that we are just beginning to enjoy thanks to the efforts of the modern hybridizers.

All the forms of *F. fulgens* are truly spectacular for their growth and flowers and this is probably my favourite form. The flowers are over 10cm (3in) long and borne in great tresses, at the tips of the long but strong stems. The tube of the flowers is salmon orange, the sepals orange with dull green tips and the petals vivid orange-scarlet. The large velvety textured leaves are light green. Many times I have seen enormous specimens of this fuchsia grown in large pots – a truly spectacular sight. Wait until this fuchsia has been in flower for a while and you will get seed pods the size of green grapes; perhaps not as tasty, but then you do not get such lovely flowers on a vine!

FUCHSIA

F. GLAZIOVIANA

FUCHSIA

F. PANICULATA

FUCHSIA

HERALD

This species fuchsia was found in 1892 in Brazil and for me has everything that you could possibly want from a fuchsia. The flowers are small and simple – the tube and sepals are pinky red. The petals are purple with a velvety sheen. *F. glazioviana* also has shiny foliage with just a hint of bronze and purple. It is short jointed when compared with most of the other species fuchsias in cultivation and is therefore an easy plant to grow. It is also a pest-free fuchsia – a characteristic that hybridizers are looking into to see if it can be bred into fuchsias of the future. *F. glazioviana* will grow into a large plant in a pot, but can also be grown as a hardy in the garden, where it will grow into a delightful bush.

Grown in the wild, *F. paniculata* can be found in natural habitats from Mexico to Panama, where it will grow to spectacular proportions. Even in a large pot this variety will achieve a height of over 1.5m (5ft) tall! The flowers are small and come in large racemes at the ends of the branches with perhaps 100 flowers on a flower head. The tube and sepals are rosy purple, the corolla lavender and the flowers are held erect. The foliage is glorious, being a deep lustrous green with a slightly serrated edge. *F. paniculata* may not be the earliest of fuchsias to flower, but once it has started you will not be disappointed. The flowers are followed by small, shiny, black berries, which birds just love!

Herald has been grown for over 150 years. It is easy to understand why, as it is such an easy fuchsia to grow. As a garden hardy it will grow to between 60cm–1m (2–3ft) tall; however, it is as a mature plant of over three years old that Herald really excels. I have several old plants of Herald, all over 10 years old and the oldest closer to 20 years. The plants are housed in large pots – which are perhaps 50cm (20in) in diameter – and they all grow to about 1.2m (4ft) tall every year, flowering for months on end. The flowers have deep red tubes and sepals and petals of a velvety purple. The foliage is a lightish green with a hint of bronze at the growing tips.

FUCHSIA

INSULINDE

Triphyllas are always popular, as not only do they give you many months of continual flowering, but their combination of flowers and foliage will take your breath away. Insulinde is one of the greatest of the modern generation of Triphyllas. Many were produced in the late nineteenth and early twentieth centuries and then few new ones appeared until the late 1980s. Now the range is increasing every year, generally with the trademark dark purple or bronze foliage and with flowers in shades of pinks, reds and oranges. Insulinde has long flowers of deep orange, borne in terminal clusters that drip with colour.

FUCHSIA

LILLIAN ANNETTS

This is a superb small- to medium-sized double-flowered fuchsia. The flowers have a waxy white tube and sepals, the full corolla has petals of a bluish lavender. Unlike some of the blue toned fuchsias, Lillian Annetts holds its colour well and looks good at any stage of its maturity. As it is a small double-flowered fuchsia, it produces a good number of flowers and is also short jointed, so it will make a lovely low growing mound if you use it for summer bedding. Plant this delightful fuchsia in a pot or garden and you will not be disappointed.

FUCHSIA

LITTLE WITCH

As its name suggests, this fuchsia has masses of small single flowers. The tube and sepals are pale lilac, the petals dark lilac – an unusual colour combination for a fuchsia. The foliage is equally small and is a rich glossy green, highlighting the colours of the flowers. Little Witch will never make a large plant but will always be a talking point in your pots or in the garden. In order to get the best results from Little Witch, grow it in a slightly shadier spot that usual; not only will it grow well, but the small and delicate looking flowers will illuminate the area around it.

FUCHSIA

LOTTIE HOBBIE

FUCHSIA

MARIN GLOW

FUCHSIA

MARTIN'S YELLOW SURPRISE

This is perhaps the best known of the encliandras and well deserves to be as popular as it is. Lottie Hobbie's small flowers are less than 2.5cm (1in) long and are a deep rose to red in colour. The equally small foliage is a dark glossy green. Lottie Hobbie is a really tough fuchsia that will survive hard winters in the garden; indeed, if there are no frosts it will often flower right the way through the winter. It will grow to between 60cm (2ft) and 1m (3ft) in the garden. In pots where its root run is perhaps a little more restricted, it can still grow into a large plant very quickly. Like all the Encliandras, Lottie Hobbie is ideal for growing around wire or plastic shapes.

In order to have a really good fuchsia collection, you need plants that go right across the spectrum of colours available. Even though this variety has been around for many years, in terms of colour there is nothing that comes anywhere near it! The large single flowers have a crisp white tube and sepals and the petals are violet with perhaps a little white area at the base. Marin Glow is a strong grower and also produces a lot of flowers for many months during the summer. It will grow into an excellent plant for pots and tubs and can be used for great effect for summer bedding, either as a contrast to other colours or as part of a glorious symphony of purples and violets.

This is an excellent inter-specific hybrid, a cross between *F. pilaloensis* and *F. fulgens* which consistently yields fantastic flowers. The tubes are long and pale peach, the sepals are green. The petals are the part that gives the plant its name, being a greeny-yellow in colour. Depending on the light, they will sometimes seem more yellow than at other times. In full flower this plant is quite an extraordinary sight: the leaves have a velvety look to them, and with the yellowish green flowers in addition it will certainly attract attention. Martin's Yellow Surprise is ideal for summer bedding or growing in a pot or tub. Persevere with this wonderful fuchsia and you will get incredible results.

FUCHSIA

NAUGHTY NICOLE

FUCHSIA

NEOPOLITAN

FUCHSIA

PHYLLIS

This was a fuchsia that we were able to release at our nursery, and the colours of this wonderful double are guaranteed to light up any hanging container or window box. The tube is white, the sepals are pale pink and the full double petals are pale violet, splashed pink. The flowers are really large and exotic and the plant will positively drip with them when it is in bloom. Mick Allsop generally names his seedlings after members of his family, so also keep a look out for Trully Treena, Heavenly Hayley and Gorgeous Gemma, all of which are large-flowered double fuchsias ideal for hanging baskets. All of them are strong growing plants with wonderfully exotic and absolutely enormous flowers. Margaret Slater is great for hanging baskets and Edith is another great hardy.

Clark, 1984. This is an example of a very select group of Encliandra fuchsias. It is one of the seven fuchsias that to me have a very distinctive perfume reminiscent of daffodils in early spring. However, be warned that probably only 50% of people will actually be able to smell its delicate perfume! Neopolitan has flowers that are less than 1cm (^{1}/$_2$in) long. They open white, turn to pink and then gradually go red – so that at any one time you can have flowers of many different hues all out at the same time, which can create quite a stir. As with all the plants in the Encliandra group, the growth of this variety can be a little wayward and straggly, but nevertheless it is well worth growing. Neopolitan was the first fuchsia that I grew around a hoop and it was then that I noticed the plant's delicate perfume.

Phyllis has to be one of the best hardy fuchsias that is widely grown; it will survive very hard winters and will also grow well in full sun, even flowering in these conditions. The flowers are semi double and the tube and sepals are waxy rose; the petals are rose. Phyllis grows to over 1m (3ft) tall and will flower for many months, making a great feature in a bed of either fuchsias alone or together with mixed plantings. Phyllis was named after the sister of the late Margaret Slater, who was for so many years the undisputed queen of fuchsias in the United Kingdom. Other fuchsias named after this famous fuchsia family include Margaret Brown, a hardy variety, President Margaret Slater, which is ideal for hanging baskets, and Edith, another very good hardy.

FUCHSIA

PIPER'S VALE

FUCHSIA

POPSIE GIRL

FUCHSIA

RUBY WEDDING

The east of England has produced many great triphylla hybridizers and growers, and this is one of those bred by one of the best – Brian Stannard. Piper's Vale has tube, sepals and corolla all of a rich orangey-red colour. The flowers are typically Triphylla, with the long tube and short sepals. Turn the flowers of this fuchsia for a closer inspection and you will see that the sepals have an unusual pale creamy white underside. Piper's Vale is also unusual for Triphyllas in that it has a lax growth, so not only can it be grown in a pot, but you can also grow it in a hanging basket, where it will trail. Like all the triphylla types, it will grow well in a really sunny position.

Dowell, 1990. I was first handed a cutting of this fuchsia at a show in the late 1980s, and Mrs Dowell was interested to know if I would be able to introduce her fuchsia. We had a long chat, and a few years later Popsie Girl was introduced. The foliage of this fuchsia is a mixture of shades – cream, grey, pink and green – combining to make a fine show even before there are flowers. Popsie Girl is a single with a creamy orange tube and sepals; the petals are rich orange, and as the foliage is light in colour the flowers do not seem as dark an orange as they might otherwise. As a foliage fuchsia Popsie Girl flowers really well. Plant it either on its own in a basket or mixed in with other plants for a wonderfully colourful effect.

This is one of the great fuchsias of recent years – outstanding in many ways. Firstly, the flowers: the tube and sepals are ruby and the corolla of this double-flowered fuchsia is a rich red. The flowers are large and a really bright colour.

Ruby Wedding is a strong grower, and the first time I ever saw it in a wall basket it was over 1.2m (4ft) wide. It created a great stir at the fuchsia show where it was on display. However, Ruby Wedding is an adaptable plant and has quite a stiff growth for a hanging basket, so it can look equally good in a pot or as part of a summer bedding display. Ruby Wedding is a fuchsia for all seasons and positions in your garden. Look out as well for the other anniversary fuchsias – Silver Anniversary and Golden Wedding, or even Happy Wedding Day.

FUCHSIA

TADDLE

FUCHSIA

THALIA

FUCHSIA

TOM WEST

I really had to include this fuchsia in this group as it was named after me by my late father. As a child I could not say my name as 'Carol' – it came out as 'Taddle', and the name has stuck. Taddle was a chance seedling taken from a batch of seeds that we grew from a seed pod found in the garden; all were grown on for several years before my father chose two that he thought were good enough to be released – Taddle and Mipam, which he named after my mother. The tube and sepals of the single flower are deep rose, the petals are creamy white. Taddle can be grown into an excellent standard – it has a vigorous upright growth, but can be equally well utilised as a plant for pots or summer bedding.

Thalia is a fuchsia that really should be in every grower's collection. It is probably the greatest of all the Triphylla fuchsias – strong growing and incredibly floriferous. Thalia has dark purple and green foliage which makes the deep orange flowers almost glow. In full flower there may be 10 to 15 flowers in every terminal cluster of flowers – quite a sight! Triphyllas love the hot spots in the garden, so use them well.

Thalia can be grown as a bush in a pot or tub or as part of a summer bedding display – but do bring it into somewhere frost free for the winter. If you enjoy a challenge, try growing Thalia as a standard: it will be fun to do and it will look superb if you are successful.

It is believed that Tom West was a sport from a great hardy fuchsia called Corallina; grow Corallina, and it will frequently sport to give plants similar to Tom West. Tom West has the most amazing foliage: the young growth is the most vivid, coloured with shades of grey, green, cream and pink. Grow Tom West in a sunny spot and the colours will become increasingly vivid; in the shade the colours are more muted. A great fuchsia is an adaptable one, and that is true of Tom West; it looks superb in a hanging basket or window box, or use it for summer bedding or as a hardy. The flowers of Tom West have deep crimson tubes and sepals and a single corolla of deepest purple.

FUCHSIA

WALZ JUBELTEEN

FUCHSIA

WAPENVELD'S BLOEI

FUCHSIA

WAVENEY GEM

This is a fuchsia that really shines: the colours are almost luminous. The tube and sepals are very pale pink, the corolla – which flares out to a slight saucer shape – is pink with a hint of orange. The flowers are also upward looking and the quantity of flowers on this plant at any one time can be amazing. The plant will also keep on flowering for many months. The names of the WALZ family of fuchsias are always rendered in upper case as they are named after the grandchildren of the hybridizer – so this is not a spelling error!

WALZ Jubelteen is another highly adaptable fuchsia and can be grown into a superb standard as the growth is so vigorous and upright. It will also make an excellent plant for tubs and pots.

A plant of this wonderful fuchsia in full flower will look like a mass of small twinkling stars, with hundreds of flowers all appearing at once. The tube and sepals are rose red, the petals are orangey red. The small flowers come in clusters and the weight of all these tiny flowers can mean that this plant may be grown in a basket or in a pot or container. The foliage has a sheen to it and emphasizes the brightness of this plant. Wapenveld's Bloei is a strong grower and will produce a large number of shoots, so this is a fuchsia that can be grown into a shape, or maybe even a pillar.

I remember the first time that I saw this fantastic fuchsia – it had been grown in a large basket and I had never seen anything quite like it before. Waveney Gem is a single; the tube and sepals are white and the petals violet. It is a strong grower, producing lots of side shoots and an abundance of flowers.

Waveney Gem is perhaps the most adaptable fuchsia that I have both known and grown. It will perform brilliantly in baskets and window boxes, as a standard, as a pillar, or in any other shape that you care to try. Whatever you choose to do with it, Waveney Gem will not let you down. This really is a gem of a plant which should be in the collection of all fuchsia growers.

NEW STYLES IN FUCHSIA FLOWERS

One of the first great colour breakthroughs in the world of fuchsias, and quite a dramatic one at the time, was the production of the first white tube and sepals found in Venus Vitrix, which was introduced in 1840. It is still a most unusual flower. Following on from this came the introduction of orange flowers and many variations on existing colours, which have since resulted in some incredible combinations of colour, size and shape.

It was not until the 1980s that hybridizers in Holland tried all kinds of crosses between species and triphyllas, and species and cultivars. Amazing things started to happen and the claret and burgundy-coloured fuchsias appeared. These have opened a whole new world of colour that we are only just starting to explore. Hybridizers are still searching for the truly yellow flower. *F. procumbens* from New Zealand has yellow within its flower, but it is genetically so far removed from the rest of the fuchsias that it is virtually impossible to cross it with any other flower. Over the years, several cultivars have appeared with yellow in them, but they have never been released as they have always been weak growers or have had other problems. Time will tell whether the dream of a yellow flower is ever realized and whether we will like it when we find it. Some hybridists are on the trail of other colour combinations – the pure orange double, for example. All the current ones have a fair degree of pink in them, as well as orange. Others are hunting for a flower with blue petals that do not fade to a washed-out lilac colour.

The angle at which the sepals are held varies according to the individual cultivar.

Above: *Fuchsiade 88 was one of the first burgundy singles to be released. It has an unusually stiff, upright growth and an abundance of flowers. It also makes an excellent hardy planted in the garden, as it is remarkably tough.*

If you examine the petals closely, you will see that they are almost diamond-shaped.

Above: *Rina Felix is one of the more unusual crosses. The shape of the flowers and the growth habit have many triphylla characteristics. However, the flowers are a new triphylla colour.*

Mood Indigo has an
extraordinary growth
habit. It is one of the most
rampant growers and
will fill a hanging basket
with great ease.

Above: Haute Cuisine is a good-sized burgundy
double, and ideal for a hanging basket. It opens
as an incredibly dark flower and fades to an
attractive lighter shade.

Right: Mood Indigo
is perhaps the most
attractive of the
burgundy fuchsias, as the
white makes a delightful
contrast with the unusual
colour of the petals.

ENCLIANDRAS

If you ever get bored with the large and traditional looking fuchsias, then take the time to explore some of the simple and small flowers of the Encliandras. They are easy to grow and versatile. A number of them have a delicate perfume; look out for Neopolitan, James Travis and Little Catbells for the strongest scents!

Encliandras are another group of fuchsias that deserve a closer examination. They have the most delightful small flowers, perfect in every detail, but never more than about 1.25cm (0.5in) long and often considerably shorter! As a group, they originated in Mexico and Central America and have a shrubby type of growth. Planted in the garden, they will make an enchanting variant in a hardy bed or in a

Above: Cinnabarina is an example of the perfection of these tiny flowers. In this case, they are less than 1cm (0.4in) long and, as in most encliandras, the flowers arise from the axils of the leaves along much of the stem.

Below: F. x bacillaris is closely related to the original encliandras from Mexico and Central America. It is thought that all the other encliandras have been crossed from this type.

Left: Encliandras in the wild and in pots have a characteristic shrubby growth and will be covered in a multitude of small flowers for many months. Many of them will prove hardy when planted in the garden.

Neapolitan is one of the more unusual fuchsias. At any one time it will have delicately perfumed, red, pink and white flowers.

Above: *A closer view of the exquisite flowers of Neapolitan. These flowers are red, which means they are fully mature.*

Above: *F. x bacillaris flowers are a lovely bright rose and, like all the encliandras, have a disproportionately large stigma.*

Above and bottom left: *Microchip is an interesting new hybrid with a wiry growth habit and masses of small, bicolored flowers that are unusual among the encliandras. It also has much paler leaves than most encliandras. The only true white-flowered encliandra is F. hidalgensis, which is a particularly rampant grower.*

summer bedding arrangement. A number of them are hardy and will survive the winter planted out in the ground in cool temperate climates. However, their greatest attraction must be their flowers. Look at them closely and you will find little jewels shining among the foliage.

The colour range of encliandras is not vast, but the assorted shades of white, pink, red and orange that are available are more than sufficient. Much hybridization has been carried out to try and widen the range, with some success. In the wild, many natural crosses have occurred, as the species of this plant may occur with female-only or male-only flowers and some will be complete flowers, with both areas functioning normally. The plants with female-only flowers rely on hummingbirds and insects to pollinate them. These pollinators will have come from another encliandra and so there is a greater chance of cross-pollination than with mixed-sex flowers on the same plant. This is why there are so many crosses in existence today.

SOME FINE ENCLIANDRAS

F. × *bacillaris*;
Cinnabarina;
F. *hemsleyana*;
F. *hidalgensis*;
F. *ravenii*;
F. *thymifolia*;
Lottie Hobby;
Miniature Jewels;
Neapolitan;
White Clove.

DISCOVERING OLD VARIETIES

Fuchsias were first introduced into Europe in the 1780s. Legend has it that a nurseryman, Mr Lee, spotted a fuchsia growing in the window of a sailor's house in Wapping, London. He recognized it as a plant with sales appeal and, having built up a stock of some 300 plants, was soon doing a brisk trade.

Since then, the fuchsia has rarely looked back and there cannot be many places where it is not found today. Many cultivars from the 1800s have tremendous strength and vigour and have survived in cultivation to this day. There is every reason to believe that people will still be growing them in 50 or 100 years time, when many of the more modern cultivars may have faded away. They must be something quite special to have survived this long and are well worth growing. There is a tendency to believe that colour breakthroughs, such as orange, are new, but they first appeared in the 1880s and are still with us today. The early hybridizers experimented more and more as the new species were discovered in South America.

Work on the hybridization of old and new varieties continues today, as modern hybridizers seek ways of extending the colour ranges of many different fuchsias in a ceaseless quest to extend and improve the already phenomenal selection of these plants. Perhaps you will wish to join them, once you have absorbed the contents of this book and discovered the wonderfully varied world of fuchsias!

Below: *Bland's New Striped was ahead of its time and looks very much like a modern introduction. In fact, this fuchsia was first seen in 1872 and it is still flourishing and very much in demand today.*

Left: *Lye's Unique was introduced in 1886 by James Lye, one of the great hybridists. The waxy white of the tube and sepals was very much his trademark. It is still popular today.*

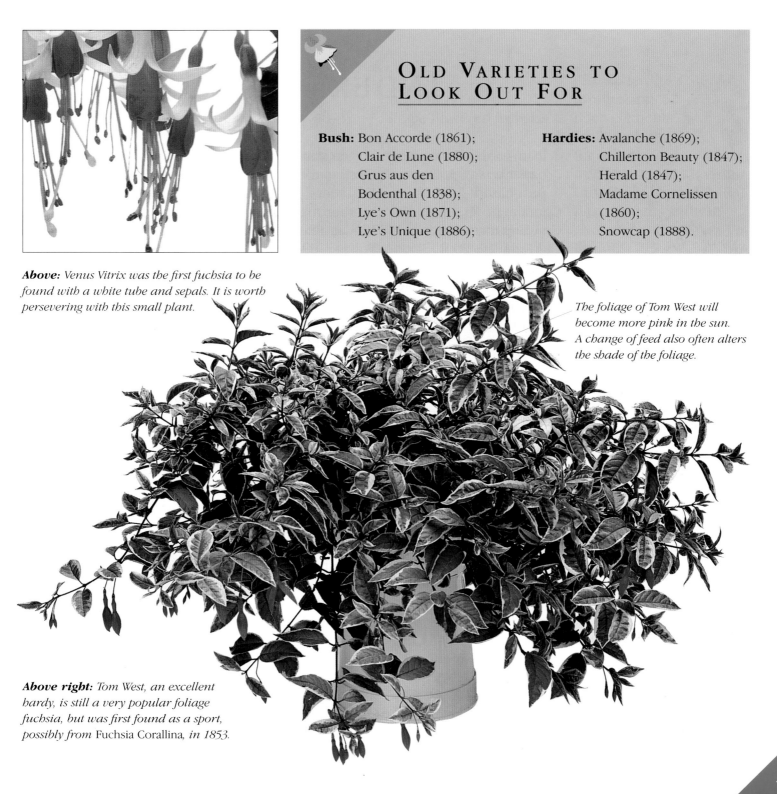

OLD VARIETIES TO LOOK OUT FOR

Bush: Bon Accorde (1861);
Clair de Lune (1880);
Grus aus den
Bodenthal (1838);
Lye's Own (1871);
Lye's Unique (1886);

Hardies: Avalanche (1869);
Chillerton Beauty (1847);
Herald (1847);
Madame Cornelissen
(1860);
Snowcap (1888).

Above: *Venus Vitrix was the first fuchsia to be found with a white tube and sepals. It is worth persevering with this small plant.*

The foliage of Tom West will become more pink in the sun. A change of feed also often alters the shade of the foliage.

Above right: *Tom West, an excellent hardy, is still a very popular foliage fuchsia, but was first found as a sport, possibly from* Fuchsia Corallina, *in 1853.*

INDEX OF PLANTS

ACKNOWLEDGEMENTS

The majority of the photographs featured in this book have been taken by Neil Sutherland and are © Salamander Books Limited. The publishers wish to thank the following photographers for providing additional photographs, credited here by page number and position on the page, as follows: (BL)Bottom left; (TR)Top right; (C)Centre; etc.

A-Z Botanical Collection: 29(BL), 124(C)
Eric Crichton: 28(BL), 65(TL, CL), 66(BR), 67(TR), 96(L)
EMAP Active: 125(C), 126(L), 129(L)
Garden Matters: 121(C)
Garden Picture Library: 26(L), 27(L, R), 30(L, R), 55(B), 123(C, R), 128(C)
John Glover: 12, 13, 62, 64, 65(R), 67(BR), 70(L, R), 71(BL, R), 97(R)
Edwin Goulding: 54(R), 55(C), 56(R), 57(T, L, R, C, B), 58(L), 59(TR, R, BR), 120(L, R), 121(L, R),
122(L, C, R), 124(L, R), 125(L, R), 126(C, R), 127(L, C, R), 128(R), 129(C, R)
S&O Mathews: 91(TL)
Peter McHoy: 110(L, R), 111(T)
Clive Nichols Garden Photography: 55(T), 66(L), 71(TL)
Photos Horticultural Picture Library: 28–9(C), 29(TR), 123(L)
Harry Smith Collection: 128(L)
Suttons: 120(C)
Thompson & Morgan: 57(TC)

The publishers would like to thank Pam Gubler and everyone at Little Brook Fuchsias
for their help in providing plants and locations for photography.